# JIMI HENDRIX EXPERIENCE
# SMASH HITS

© TM Authentic Hendrix, LLC

Arranged by Jim Schustedt and Mike Schmidt

ISBN 978-1-4768-7725-9

EXPERIENCE
HENDRIX

EXCLUSIVELY DISTRIBUTED BY

HAL•LEONARD®
CORPORATION
7777 W. BLUEMOUND RD. P.O. BOX 13819 MILWAUKEE, WI 53213

Visit Jimi Hendrix Online at
**www.jimi-hendrix.com**

Visit Hal Leonard Online at
**www.halleonard.com**

# Performance Notes

### Purple Haze

The wavy line above the tenth measure is the symbol used for vibrato. Fret the third string with your ring finger while using the palm of your left hand near the base of your index finger to rest against the bottom of the neck. Your palm will act as a fulcrum, allowing your ring finger to wiggle up and down, altering the pitch of the string. There's a bit of dissonance in the E7#9 chord. This is because the chord contains both a G note (fifth string, open) and a G# note (third string, first fret). This was Jimi's trademark chord.

### Fire

Although unusual, pick the pinches in the Intro with your index and middle fingers. This will position your thumb to pick the open fifth string. For the roll leading into the Verse, fret the "7" with your ring finger, the "6" with your middle, and the "5" with your index finger. Hold this chord shape for the entire Verse. Immediately after picking the open fifth string at the end of the roll, use your left hand pinky to lightly touch the fifth string to stop it from ringing.

The Banjo Solo modulates up a whole step to the key of A. Always use your pinky to fret the notes on the first string, 7th fret in this section. For the last note in the third and fifth measures, use your middle finger to fret the second string, 5th fret.

Like the Banjo Solo, the Outro begins in the key of A. Use the same fingerings as above for the first four measures. The last four measures modulate back to the key of G. Just shift your hand down two frets and you'll have it.

### The Wind Cries Mary

Use your fret hand index finger to barre the strings wherever possible in this song.

At the end of the first measure there is a muted backward strum. While holding the previous chord, lightly lay your fret hand pinky across all of the strings, then drag your pick hand middle finger upward across the strings.

The Banjo Solo is full of chords. Look at all the notes in each measure to determine the best left hand fingering, then fret all the notes simultaneously so the notes ring together.

### Can You See Me

The fingerings for this arrangement are pretty standard. Be aware of the time change: there is a 2/4 measure near the end of the Verse. Three measures later, notice the dots above the tab numbers: those D7#9 chords are played staccato, or short. Between each chord, slightly lift your fret hand fingers while maintaining contact with the strings. This will stop the strings from ringing between each chord. To play the staccato G chord in the first ending, use the fingers of your left hand to touch the strings immediately after they're plucked.

### Hey Joe

In the Verses, use your ring finger to barre all the notes in the Bb and C chords. This will make for a smooth transition to the chords that follow.

In the first four measures of the Banjo Solo, keep your ring finger planted on the first string.

In the Interlude, anchor your ring finger on the "3" for the entire measure. Use standard F chord fingerings in the second measure. Keep your fingers in place, then use your pinky to fret the "3" and "4" on the third string. In the third measure, fret and hold the "5" on the third string with your pinky for the entire measure; likewise, hold the "5" on the second string with your ring finger.

The first four measures of the Interlude are labeled Riff A. Substitute Riff A for what's written in the first four measures of page 22 during the third Verse. Riff A is also recalled on the repeat in the fourth Verse.

## All Along the Watchtower

Use your index finger to barre the A chord in the Intro. Continue to barre while using your middle, ring, and pinky fingers to fret the Bm chord. There are two eighth rests immediately following the Bm chords. Use your pick hand fingers to stop the strings from ringing. One measure later you'll need to employ this technique after the G chords.

For the Bm chords in the Verse, fret the "4" with your ring finger, and continue to hold the note while you play the "2" in the hammer-on/pull-off sequence with your index finger. Barre your index finger at the 2nd fret to play the recurring A chords.

The Banjo Solo has some cool "outside" notes in the second measure. Barre the first and second strings with your index finger at the 3rd fret for the first two beats, then slide your index up to the 5th fret for beat three, then slide up again to the 8th fret for beat four. The sixth measure starts the same way, but this time slide the barre up to the 6th fret for beat three, then to the 9th fret for beat four.

The notes in the Outro will test the intonation of your banjo. You may have to adjust the placement of your bridge to make the three B notes play in tune.

## Stone Free

Beginning in the third measure, there are muted strings, indicated by Xs in tab. Lift your fret hand finger off the fretboard while still maintaining contact with the string. Picking the muted string will produce a percussive click.

In the Pre-Chorus, barre your index finger for the A chords, then flatten out your ring finger on the third and fourth strings at the 7th fret. Likewise, flatten your index at the 5th fret, then alternate between these two fingers. The Chorus uses the same technique.

## Crosstown Traffic

The continuous vibrato at the beginning of the Intro is accomplished by vigorously shaking your left arm while fretting the D7#9 chord. This exaggerated motion will alter the pitch of all of the notes, which is a cool effect.

## Manic Depression

Other than being in 3/4 time, this song's pretty straightforward. Notice that the eighth notes are swung. (See "Red House" below for an explanation.)

## Remember

Each measure of the Verse is comprised of two chord shapes. Position your fingers so you can hold down all notes of the chord in beats one and two so they will ring together when picked. Often you'll be barring the strings with your index finger. Begin beat three by sliding your ring finger, then all the other notes for the remainder of the measure will be within reach. You'll want to hold your fingers down for beats three and four so the notes ring together.

Notice the staccato dots in the Bridge and Outro. Be sure to play the notes short.

## Red House

The first two measures of the Intro consist of triplet eighth notes. Play three notes of the same duration for each beat. Notice the eighth note indicator in parentheses to the right of the "Slow" tempo marking at the top of the page: this tells you to "swing" the eighth notes, or play them as a shuffle. When eighth notes are beamed together, the first one in each pair is allowed to sustain longer than normal, and the second is played shorter than normal. The long note should be sustained the same duration as the first two notes of an eighth-note triplet, while the shorter note will be sustained the same duration as the third note of a triplet.

## Foxey Lady

Like "Crosstown Traffic," this one begins with vibrato. In the fourth measure, you jump from the 2nd fret to the 14th. This lick happens often, so you'll get good at it before long. The dots above the first "2" and "14" mean they are to be played staccato.

In the fifth measure of the Banjo Solo, use your fret hand middle finger for the slide on the second string, your index finger for the "16" on the third string, and your ring finger for the "17" on the first string. Keep all three fingers down and reach for the "19" with your pinky. In the sixth measure, use your pinky for the "14" on the first string. Your index, middle and ring fingers will fret the fifth, second, and first strings respectively at the 12th fret.

# Purple Haze

**Words and Music by Jimi Hendrix**

G tuning:
(5th-1st) G-D-G-B-D

Key of E

**Intro**
**Moderately**

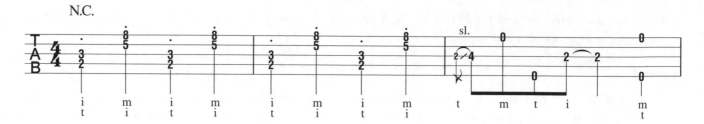

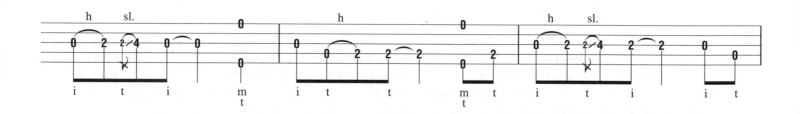

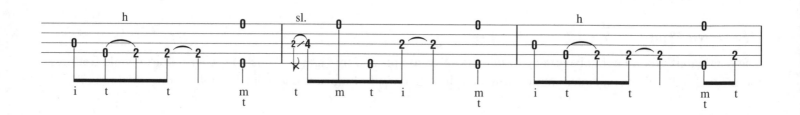

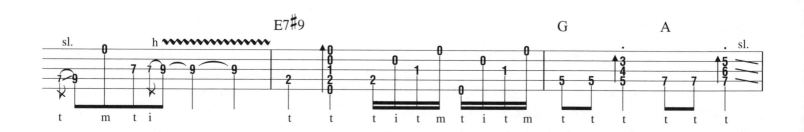

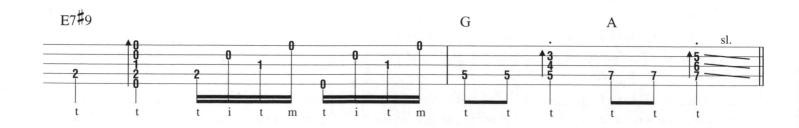

**𝄋 Verse**

1. Purple haze                   all       in    my   brain.
2., 3. *See additional lyrics*

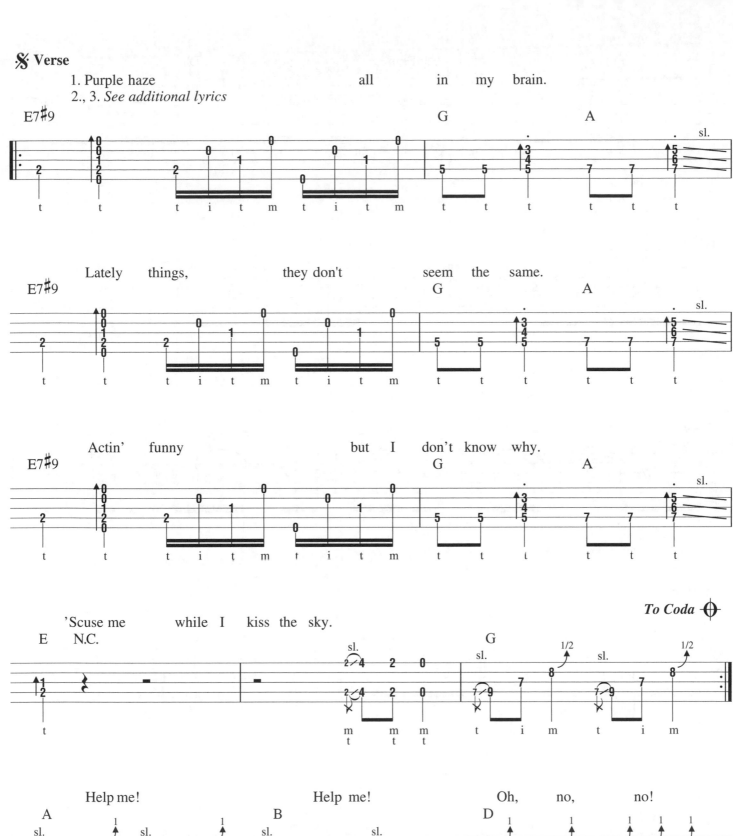

Lately   things,        they don't       seem  the  same.

Actin'  funny              but   I   don't know  why.

*To Coda* ⊕

'Scuse me      while I  kiss the sky.

Help me!                  Help me!                Oh,    no,    no!

**Banjo Solo**

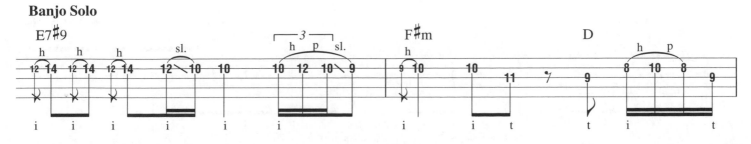

5

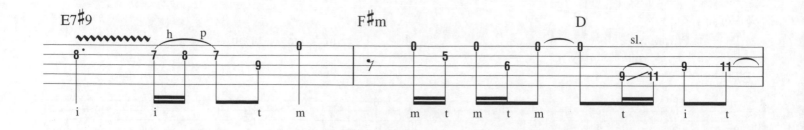

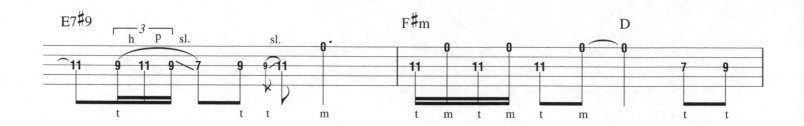

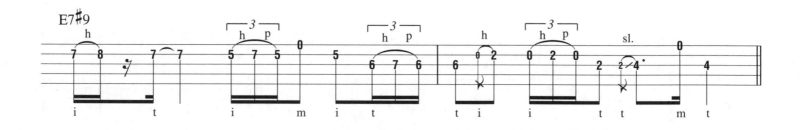

**Interlude**

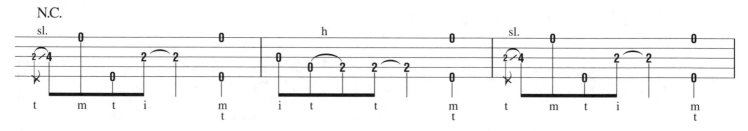

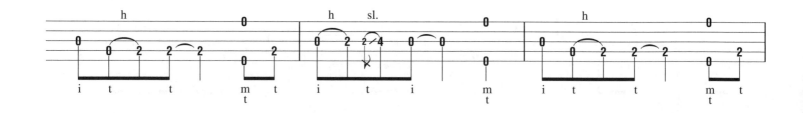

***D.S. al Coda***

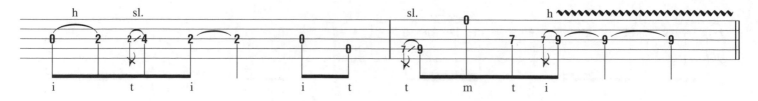

## ⊕ Coda
### Outro

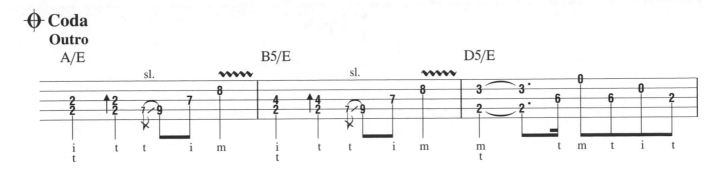

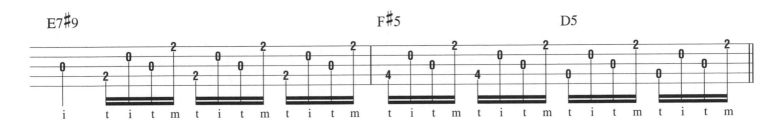

*Repeat & fade*

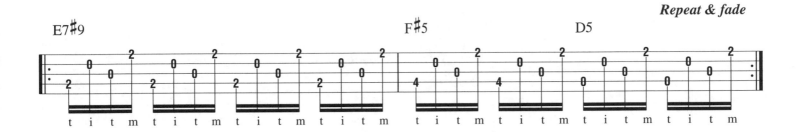

**Additional Lyrics**

2. Purple Haze is all around.
   Don't know if I'm coming up or down.
   Am I happy or in misery?
   Whatever it is, that girl put a spell on me.
   Help me! Help me!

3. Purple haze all in my eyes.
   Don't know if it's day or night.
   You've got me blowing, blowing my mind.
   Is it tomorrow or the end of time?

# Fire

**Words and Music by Jimi Hendrix**

G tuning:
(5th-1st) G-D-G-B-D

Key of G

### Intro
**Moderately fast**

N.C.

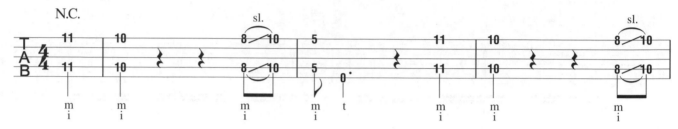

**𝄋 Interlude**
1. Alright!
2., 3. *See additional lyrics*

N.C.(G)

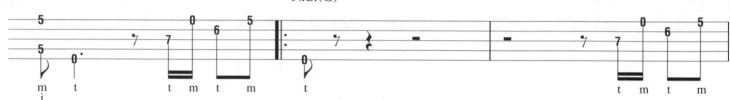

Now, dig this, baby!

**Verse**

1. You don't care for me, I don't, a,
2., 3. *See additional lyrics*

N.C.(G)

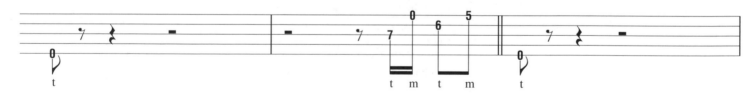

care about that. You got a new fool, ha, I like it like that.

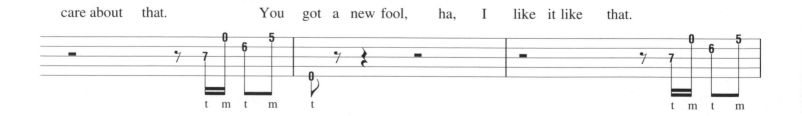

I have only one, a, burning desire,     let me stand    next to your

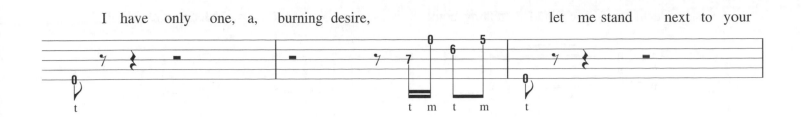

**Chorus**

fire!         Let me     stand     next to your   fire.

G                                    Fadd9

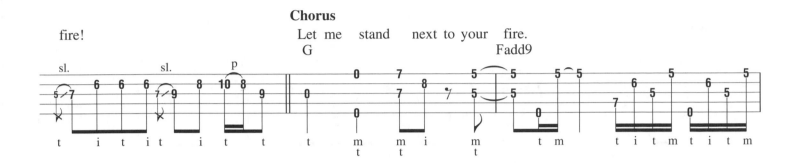

Let me     stand     next to your fire.     Whoa, let    me…         Let me     stand     next to your

G                      Fadd9                                   G

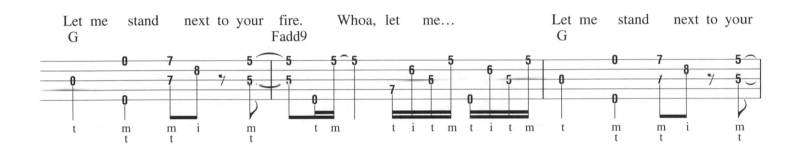

*To Coda* ⊕

fire.        Let    me…          Let me     stand     next to your   fire. Yeah, baby.

Fadd9                             G                           Fadd9

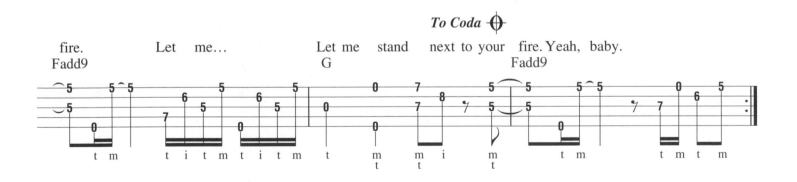

**Bridge**

Oh, move over,   Rover                      and let    Jimi take over.

G                                     Fadd9

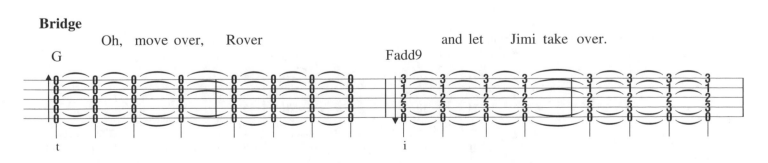

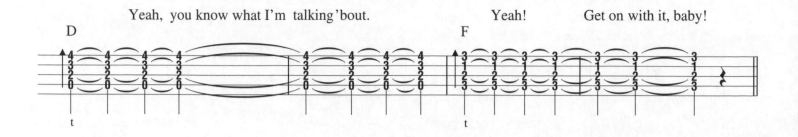

Yeah, you know what I'm talking 'bout.    Yeah!    Get on with it, baby!

Key of A
**Banjo Solo**

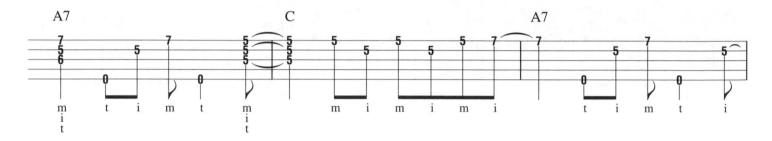

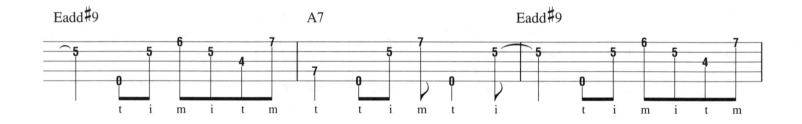

Key of G
**Interlude**

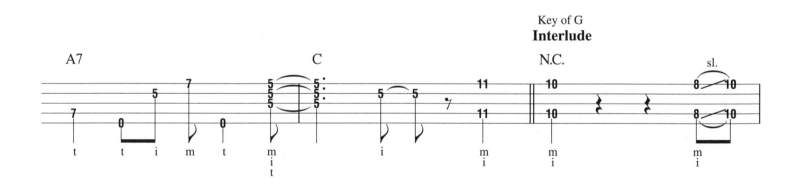

*D.S. al Coda*

That's what I'm talking 'bout.    Now dig this!

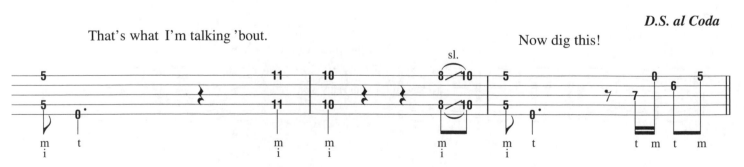

10

## ⊕ Coda

### Outro
**Key of A**

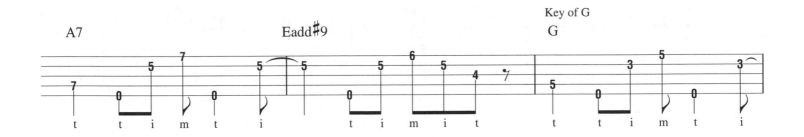

**Repeat & fade**

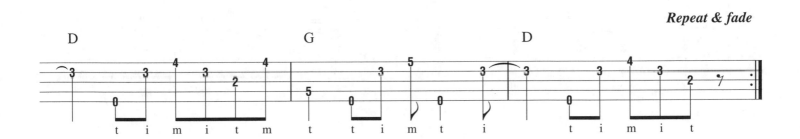

**Additional Lyrics**

Interlude 2  Listen here, baby,
         And stop acting so crazy.

Verse 2  You say your mum ain't home,
         It ain't my concern.
         Just play with me
         And you won't get burned.
         I have only one itching desire,
         Let me stand next to your fire!

Interlude 3  Ha!
         Now, listen, baby!

Verse 3  You try to gimme your money,
         You better save it, babe,
         Save it for your rainy day.
         I have only one burning desire,
         Let me stand next to your fire!

# The Wind Cries Mary

**Words and Music by Jimi Hendrix**

G tuning:
(5th-1st) G-D-G-B-D

Key of G

**Intro**
**Slow**

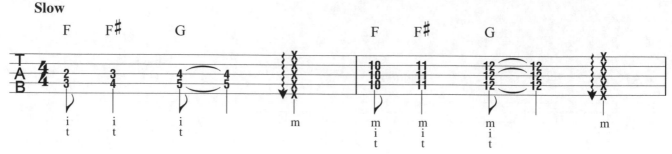

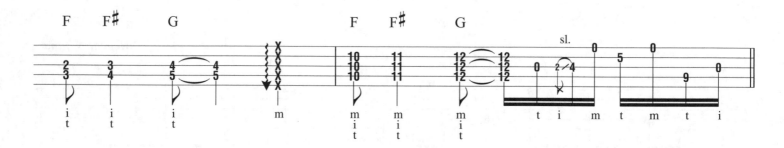

**%  Verse**

1. After all the jacks are in          their          boxes,                                        and the
2., 3., 4. *See additional lyrics*

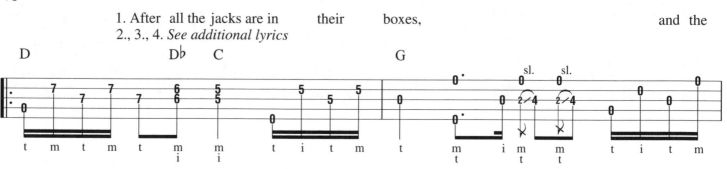

clowns                    have all          gone   to          bed,                              you can

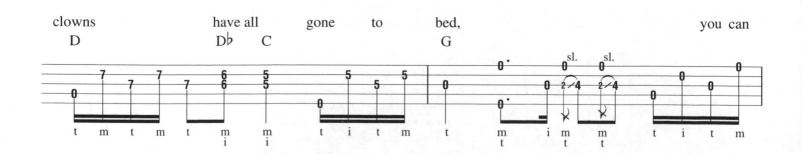

hear happiness staggering on down the street,

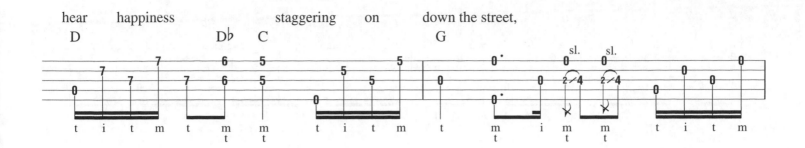

foot - prints dressed in red. And the

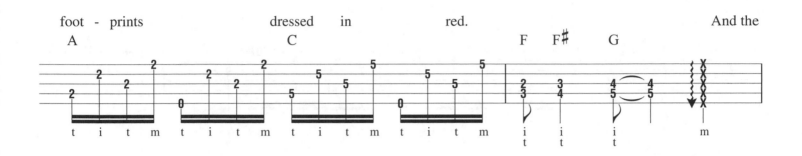

*4th time, to Coda* ⊕

wind whispers Mary.

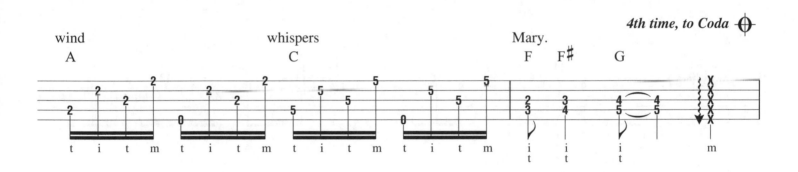

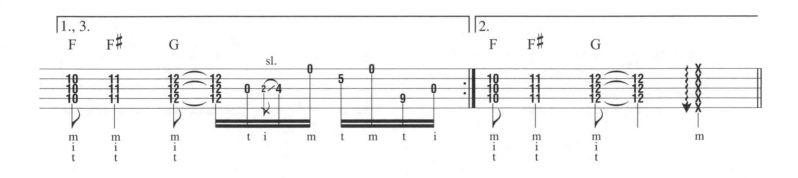

**Banjo Solo**

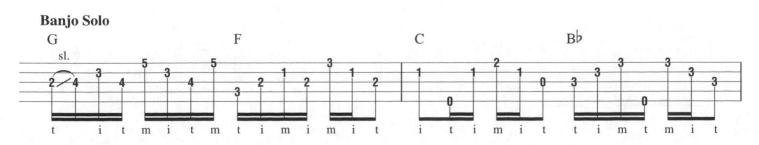

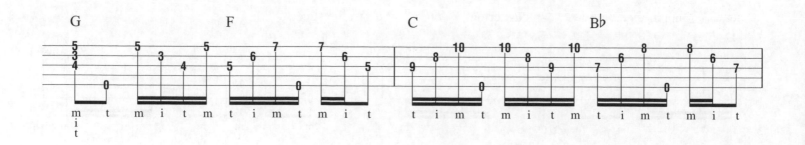

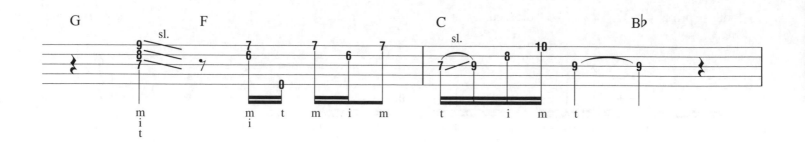

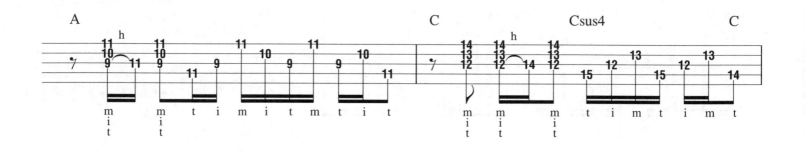

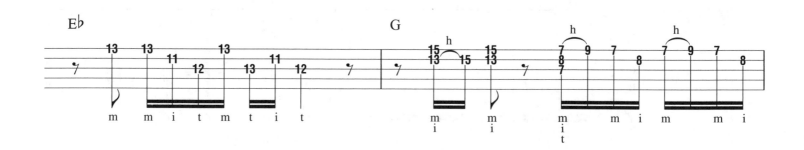

***D.S. al Coda***
***(take repeat)***

⊕ **Coda**

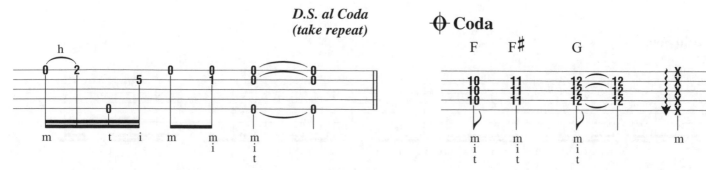

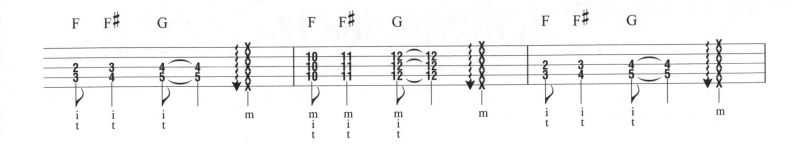

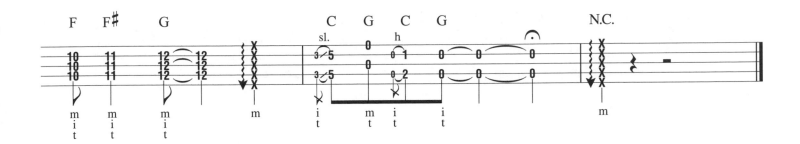

**Additional Lyrics**

2. A broom is drearily sweeping
   Up the broken pieces of yesterday's life.
   Somewhere a queen is weeping,
   Somewhere a king has no wife.
   And the wind, it cries Mary.

3. The traffic lights, they turn blue tomorrow
   And shine their emptiness down on my bed.
   The tiny island sags downstream
   'Cos the life that lived is dead.
   And the wind screams Mary.

4. Will the wind ever remember
   The names it has blown in the past?
   And with this crutch, its old age and its wisdonm,
   It whispers, "No, this will be the last."
   And the wind cries Mary.

# Can You See Me

**Words and Music by Jimi Hendrix**

G tuning:
(5th–1st) G-D-G-B-D

Key of G

**Intro**
**Moderately fast**

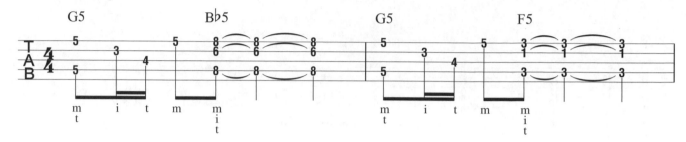

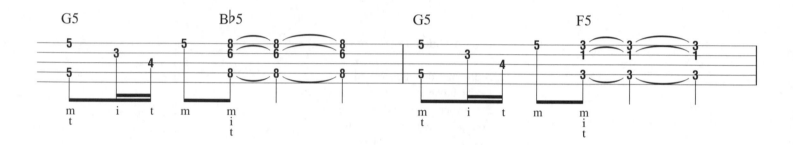

%

1. Uh, can you see me, yeah,
3. *See additional lyrics*   2., 4. *See additional lyrics*

**Verse**

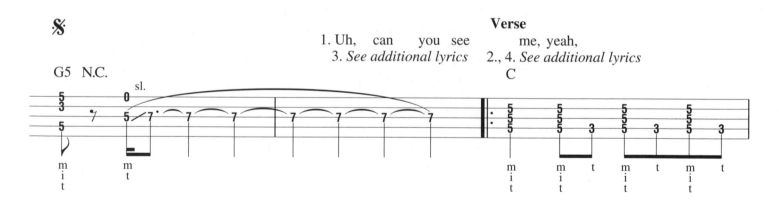

begging you on my knee?

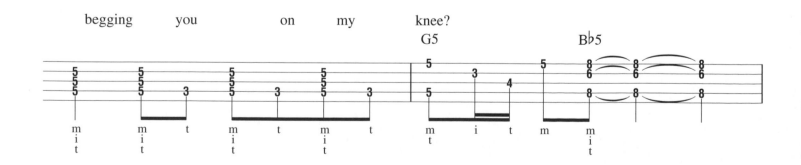

Whoa, yeah!

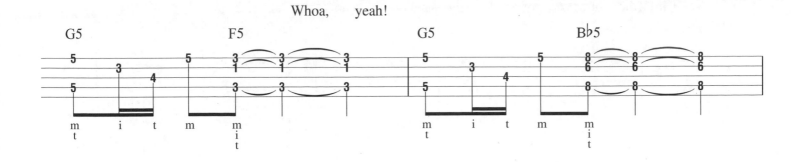

Can you see me, baby,

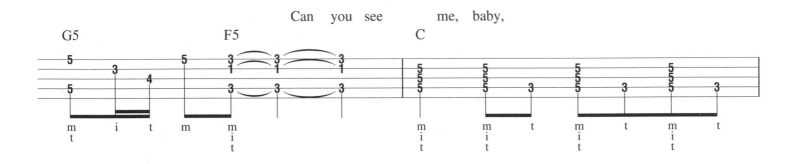

*4th time, to Coda* ⊕

begging please don't leave?

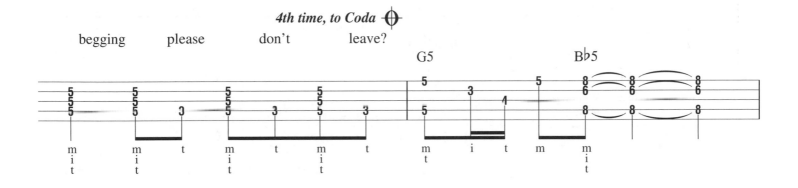

Alright.

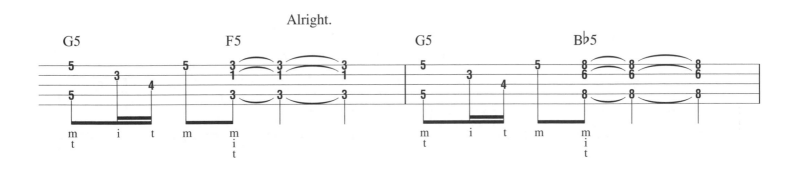

If you can see me doing that, you can

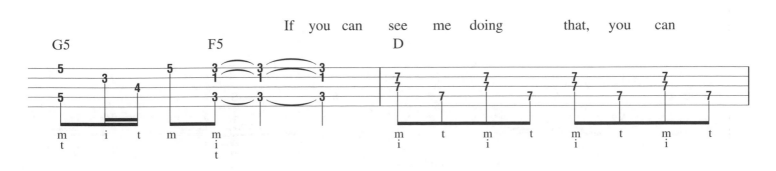

see in the future of a thousand years.

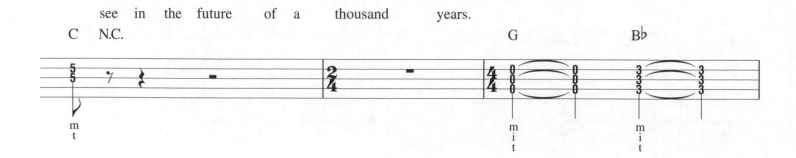

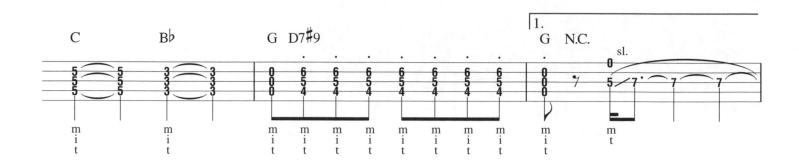

2. Uh, can you hear
4. Can you hear

**Interlude**

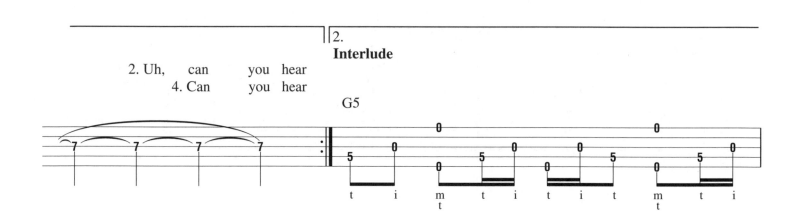

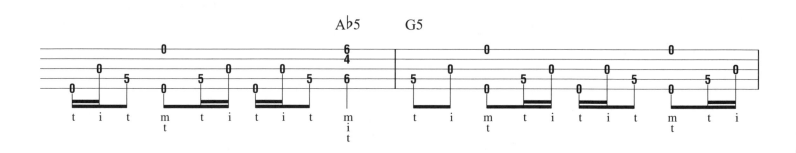

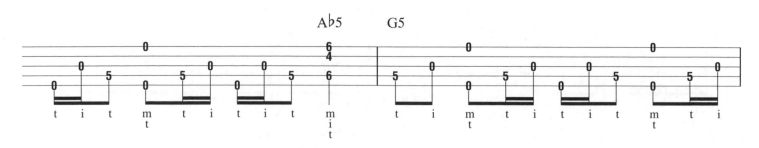

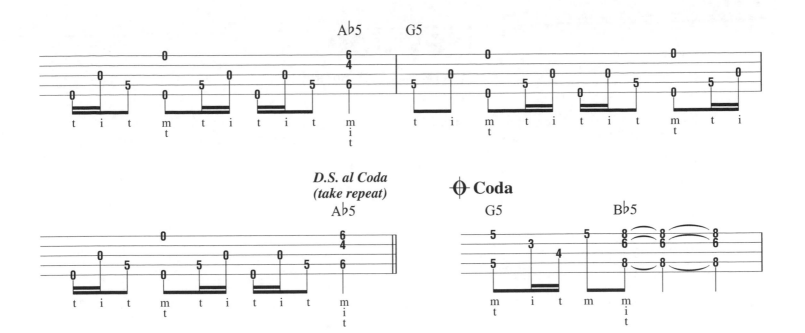

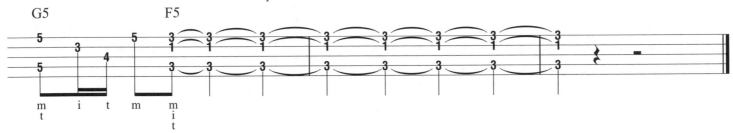

*Spoken: You can't see me.*

### Additional Lyrics

2. Uh, can you hear me, yeah,
Crying all over town?
Yeah, baby,
Can you hear me, baby,
Crying 'cos you put me down?
Let's reach up, girl.
If you can hear me doing that, you can
Hear a freight train coming from a thousand miles.

3. Ooh! Uh, can you hear me
Singing this song to you?
Ah, you better open up your ears, baby!
Can you hear me, baby,
Singing this song to you?
Ah, shucks!
If you can hear me sing,
You better come home like you 'sposed to do.

4. Can you see me?
Hey, hey!
I don't believe you can see me.
Whoa, yeah.
Can you hear me, baby?
I don't believe you can.

# Hey Joe

**Words and Music by Billy Roberts**

G tuning:
(5th-1st) G-D-G-B-D

Key of D

**Intro**
**Moderately**

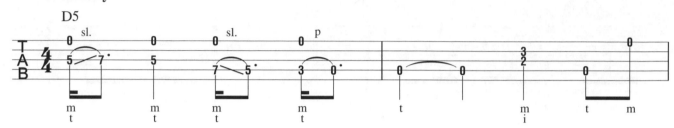

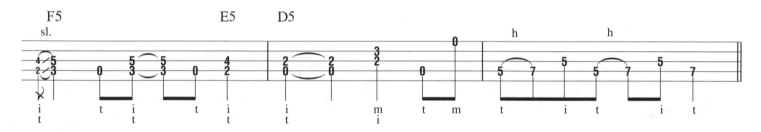

 **Verse**

1. Hey,                   Joe,                                         uh,
2., 3. *See additional lyrics*

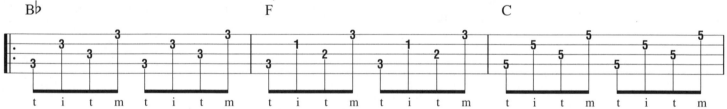

where you goin'    with that        gun in your   hand?

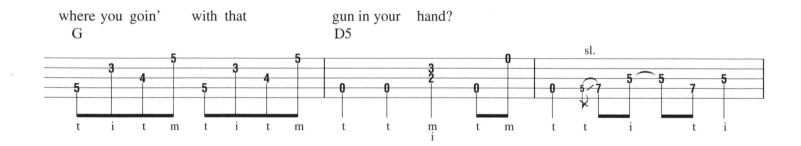

Hey,

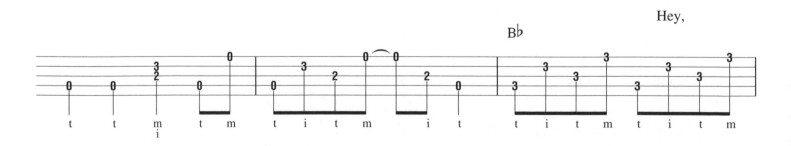

Joe,        I said,     where you goin' with that       gun

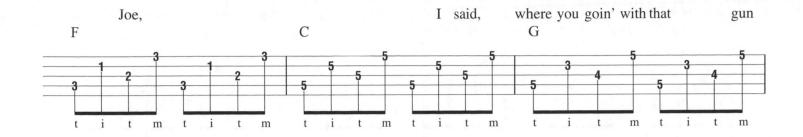

in your hand?

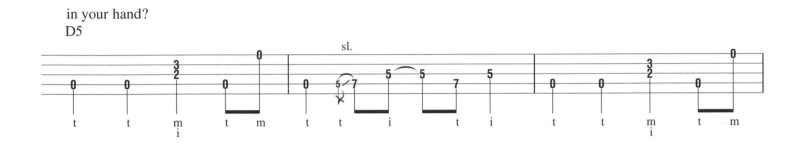

"I'm goin' down to    shoot my old lady,

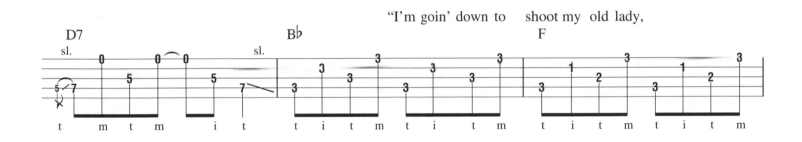

you know I   caught her messin' 'round    with another man.

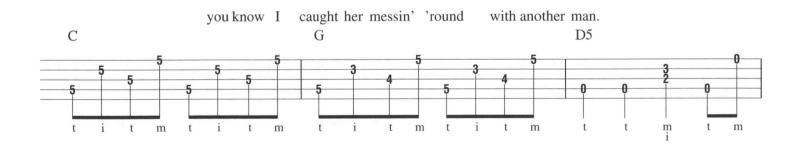

Yeah!

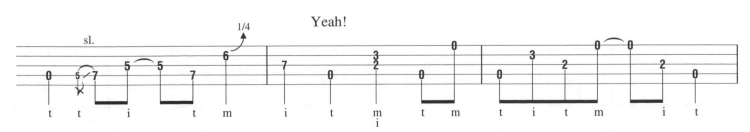

I'm goin' down to shoot my old lady,        you know I

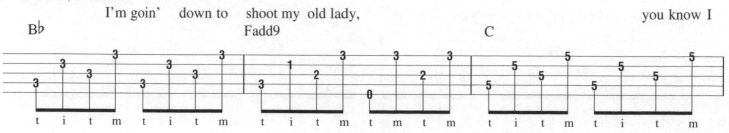

caught her messin' 'round    with   another     man.       Huh!       And that ain't

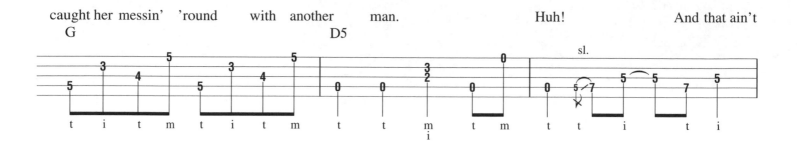

*To Coda*     |1.           |2.

too cool."          I    shot    her!

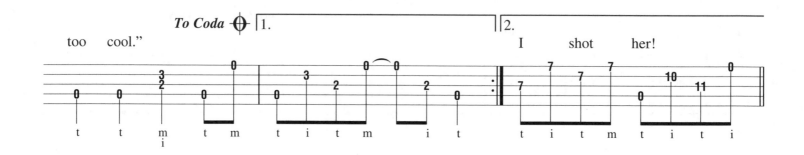

**Banjo Solo**

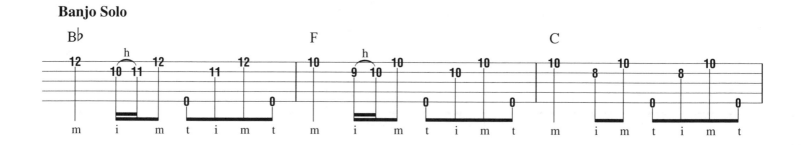

Al - right.

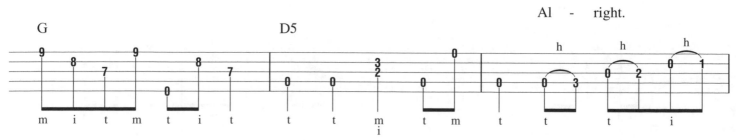

22

Shoot her one more time again. Will ya?

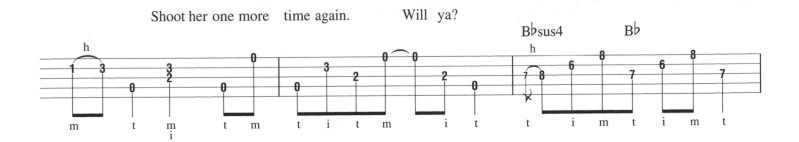

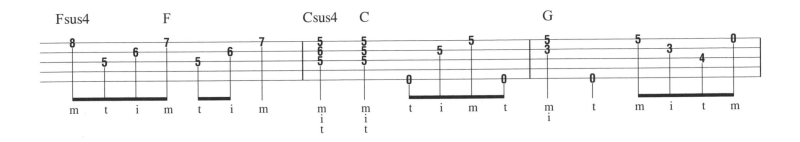

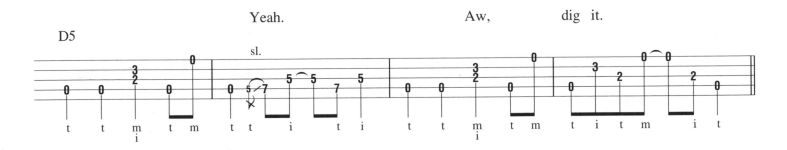

Yeah. Aw, dig it.

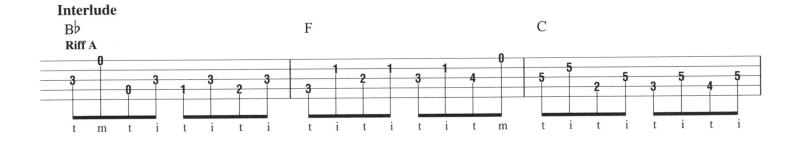

**Interlude**

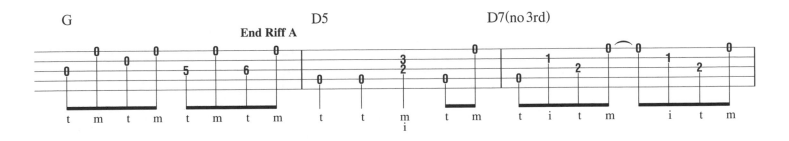

*D.S. al Coda*

Al - right.

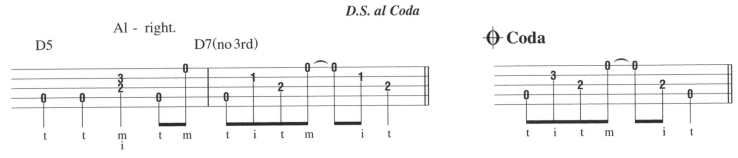

## Verse

2nd time, w/ Riff A

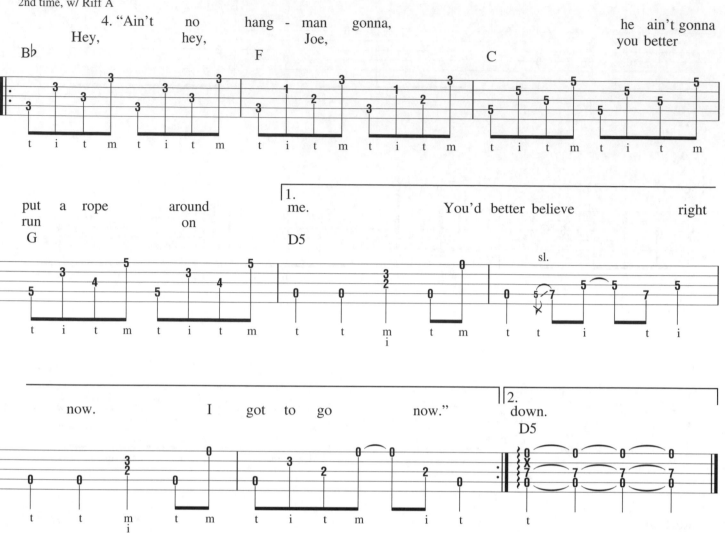

**Additional Lyrics**

2. Hey, Joe, I heard you shot your woman down,
   You shot her, now.
   Hey, Joe, I heard you shot your old lady down,
   You shot her down in the ground. Yeah!
   "Yes, I did, I shot her.
   You know I caught her messin' 'round, messin' 'round town.
   Yes, I did, I shot her.
   You know I caught my old lady messin' 'round town,
   And I gave her the gun.
   I shot her."

3. Hey, Joe, a where you gonna run to now?
   Where you gonna run to?
   Hey, Joe, I said, where you gonna run to now?
   Where you, where you gonna go? Well, dig it.
   "I'm goin' way down south, way down to Mexico way.
   Alright.
   I'm goin' way down south, way down where I can be free.
   There ain't no one gonna find me."

# Stone Free

**Words and Music by Jimi Hendrix**

G tuning:
(5th-1st) G-D-G-B-D

Key of E

**Intro**
**Moderately**

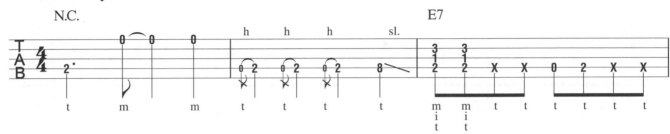

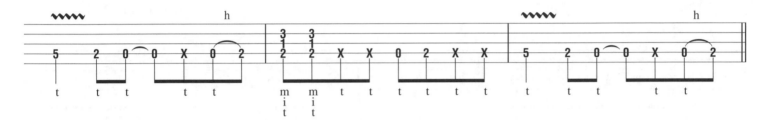

**Verse**

1. Ev'ry day in the week I'm in a dif - f'rent cit - y.
2. *See additional lyrics*

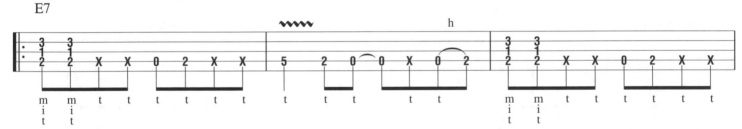

Ooh, if I stay too long the people try to

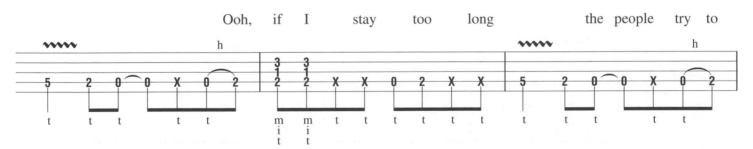

pull me down. They talk about me like a dog,

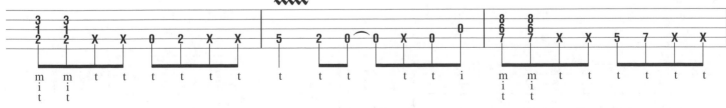

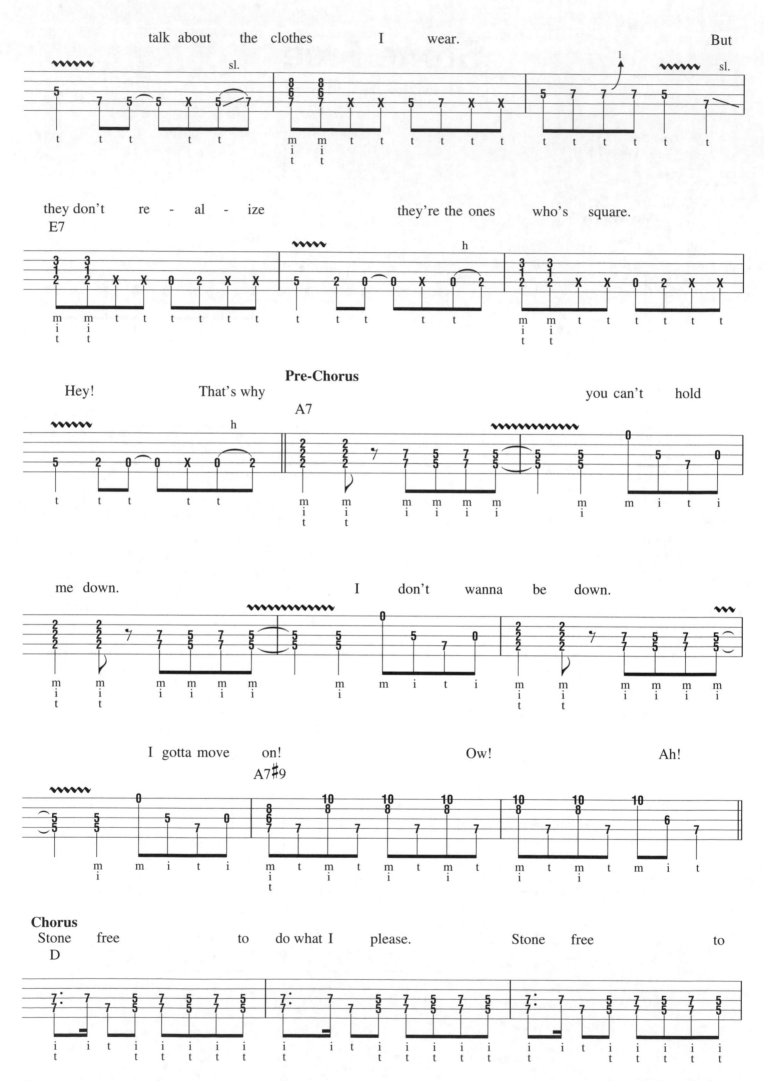

ride     the     breeze.     Stone     free!           I can't     stay!        I

got   to, got  to, got  to get away     right     now.               Yeah!

C                    A                    C                    A

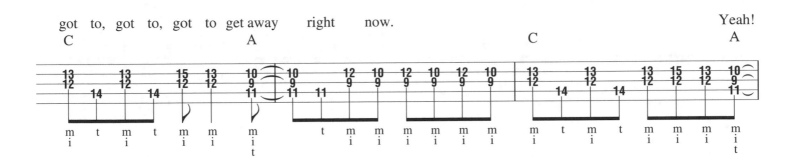

Alright!

1. **Interlude**

E7

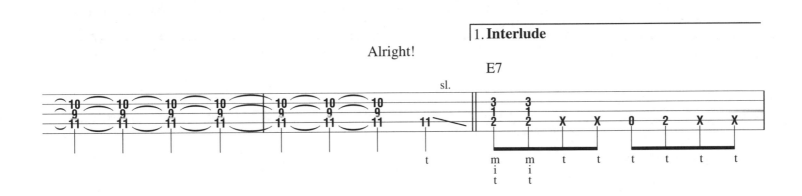

Listen to this, baby.

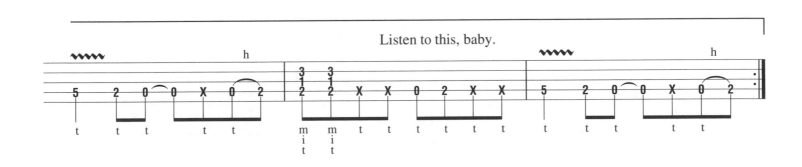

2. **Banjo Solo**

Am

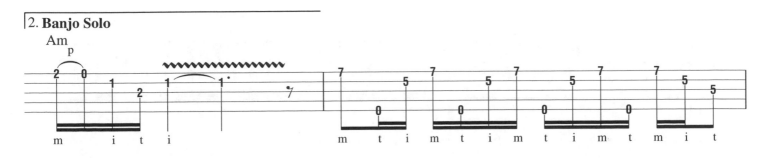

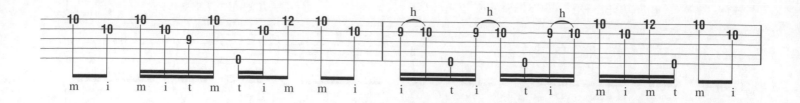

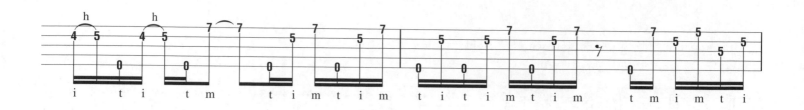

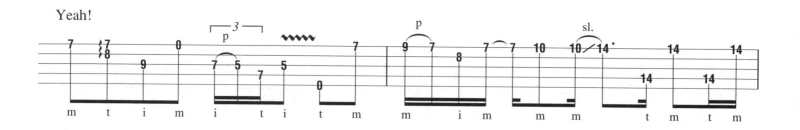

Yeah!

Aw!

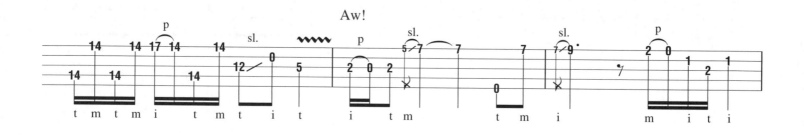

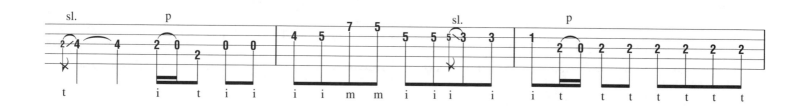

Aw!
A7#9

Yeah!

I

said,

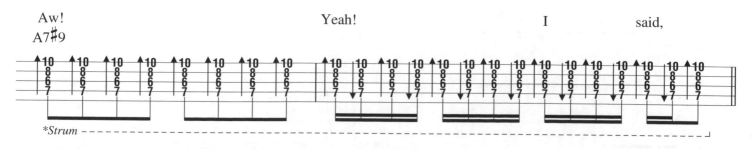

*Strum

*Use nails of right hand ring and pinky fingers for downstrums, and thumbpick for upstrums.

**Chorus**

Stone free      free              to  ride       the  breeze.

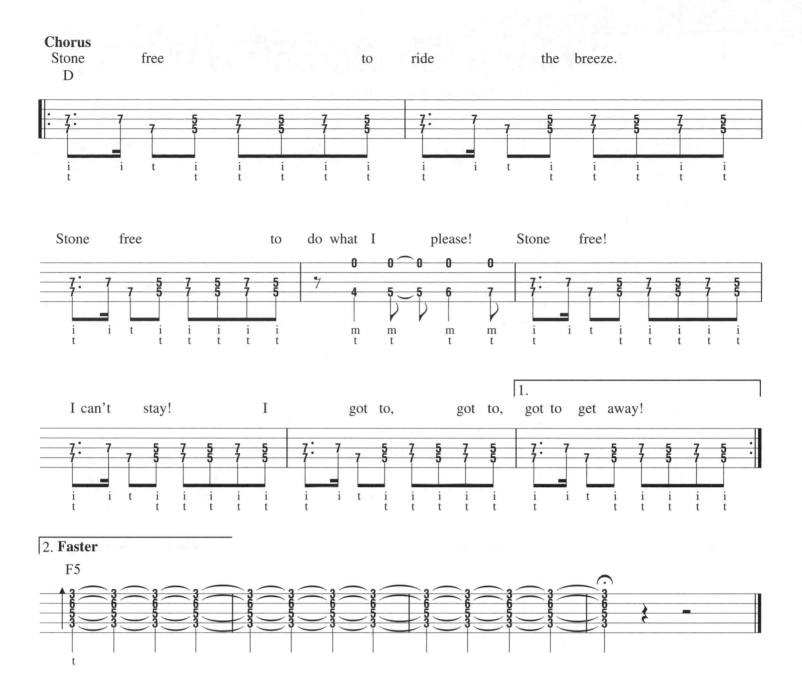

**Additional Lyrics**

2. Woman here, woman there, tryin' to keep me in a plastic cage.
   But they don't realize it's so easy to break.
   Oh, but sometimes I get, uh, hot!
   I could feel my heart kinda runnin' hot.
   That's when I've got to move before I get caught.

Pre-Chorus 2  Hey! That's why,
   Listen to me, baby,
   You can't hold me down.
   I don't want to be tied down.
   I gotta be free! Ow!

Chorus 2  I said, stone free to do what I please!
   Stone free to ride the breeze!
   Stone free! I can't stay!
   Got to, got to, got to get away!
   Yeah! Ow!
   Turn me loose, baby!

# All Along the Watchtower

**Words and Music by Bob Dylan**

G tuning:
(5th-1st) G-D-G-B-D

Key of Bm

**Intro**
   **Moderately**

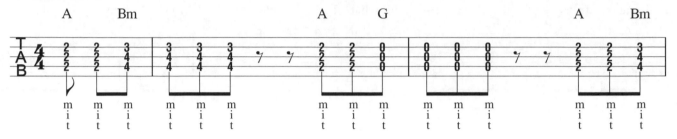

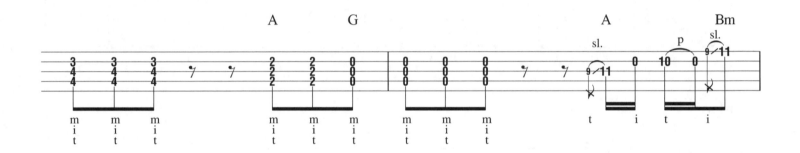

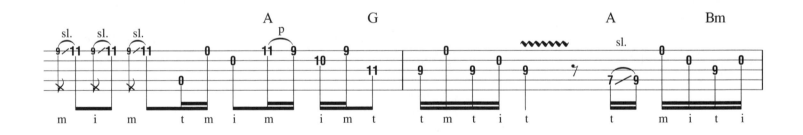

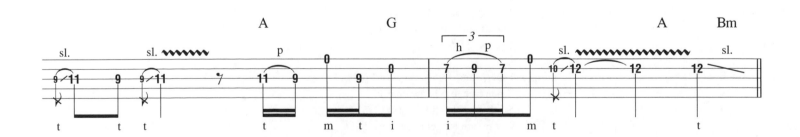

% **Verse**

1. There must be some kind a way outta here
2., 3. *See additional lyrics*

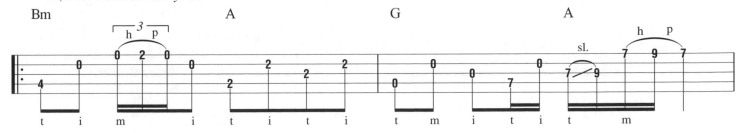

say the joker to the thief.

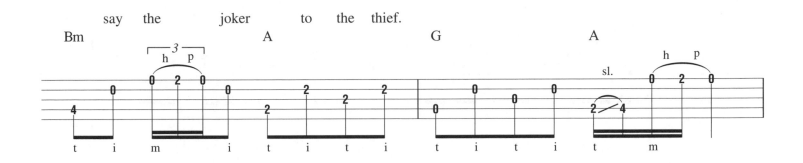

There's too much confusion, ah.

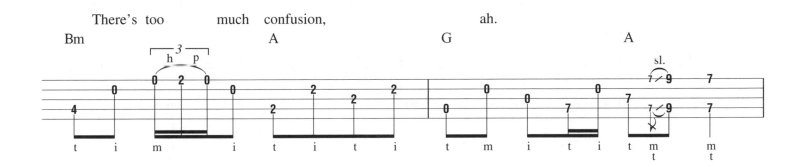

I can't get no relief.

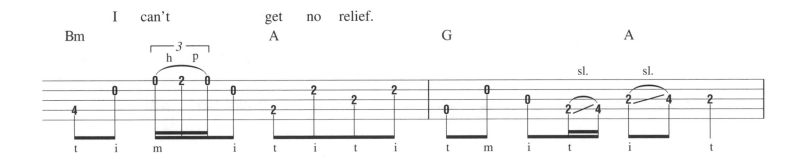

Business men, they, ah, ah, drink my wine.

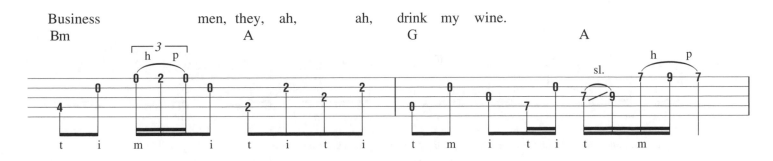

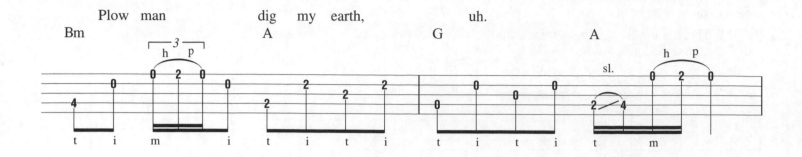

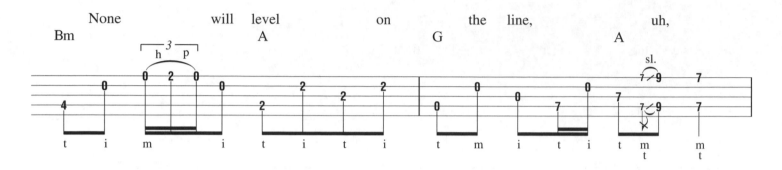

*3rd time, to Coda*

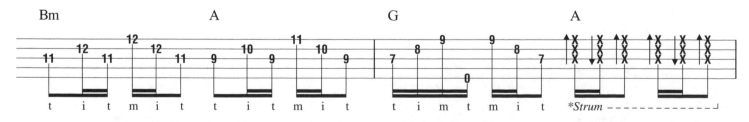

**Banjo Solo**

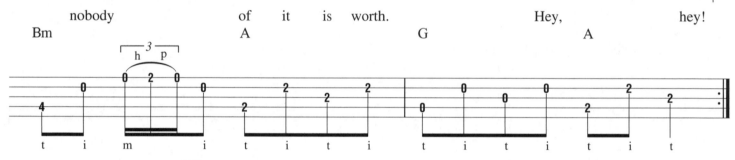

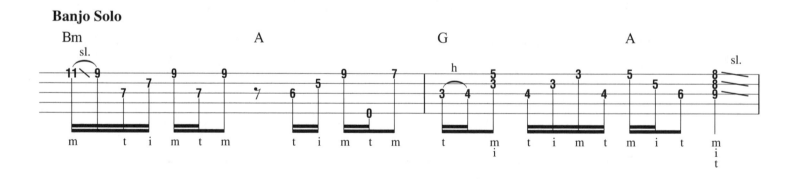

*Use nails of right hand ring and pinky fingers for downstrums, and thumbpick for upstrums.

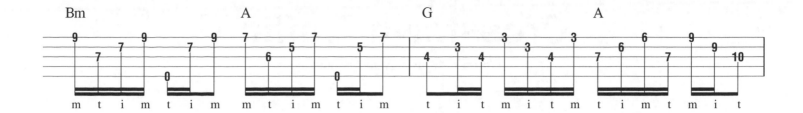

*D.S. al Coda*

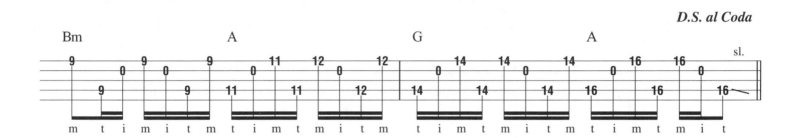

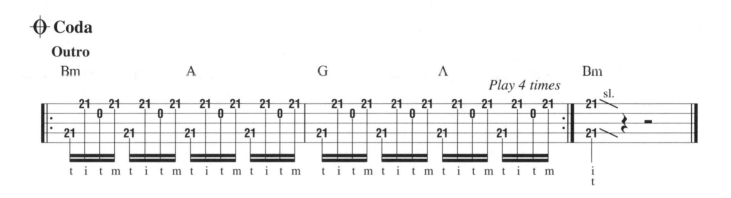

**Additional Lyrics**

2. No reason to get excited,
   The thief, kindly spoke.
   There are many here among us
   Who feel that life is but a joke.
   But, uh, but you and I, we've been through all that,
   And this is not our fate.
   So let us not talk falsely now,
   The hour is getting late, ah.
   Hey!

3. Well, all along the watchtower
   Princes kept the view
   While all the women came and went,
   Bare feet servants too.
   Well, ah, outside in the cold distance
   A wild cat did growl.
   Two riders were approachin'
   And the wind began to howl.
   Hey!

# Crosstown Traffic

**Words and Music by Jimi Hendrix**

G tuning:
(5th-1st) G-D-G-B-D

Key of D

### Intro
**Moderately**

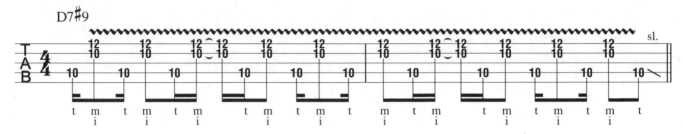

Do, do, doodle, do, do, do.

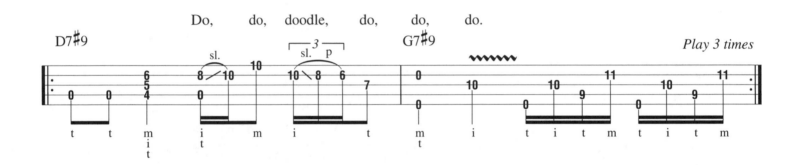

Do, do, do, do, do, do,   do, do, do, do.

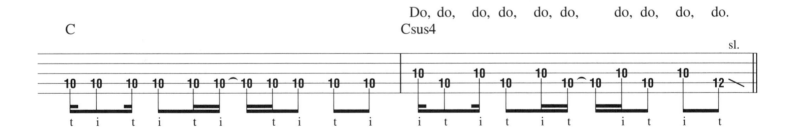

### Verse

1. You jump in front of my car when you,   you know all the time   that, ah,
2. *See additional lyrics*

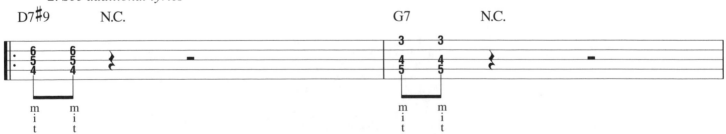

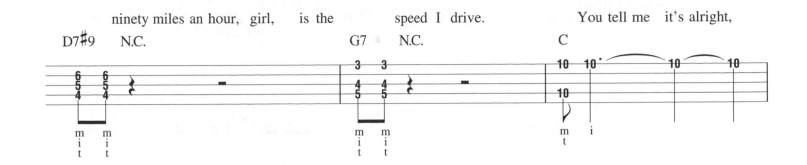

ninety miles an hour, girl, is the speed I drive. You tell me it's alright,

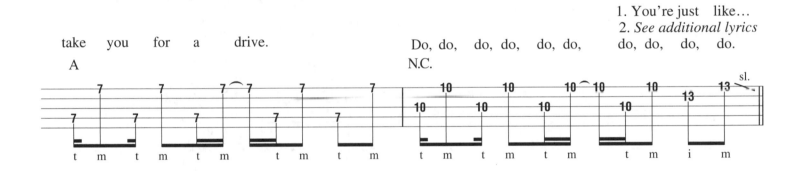

you don't mind a little pain. You say you just want me to

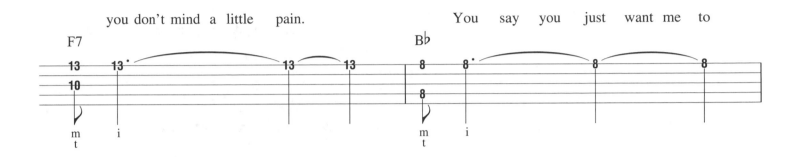

1. You're just like…
2. *See additional lyrics*

take you for a drive. Do, do, do, do, do, do, do, do, do, do.

**Chorus**

So hard to get through to you.

Cross - town traffic. Do, do, doodle, do, do, do.

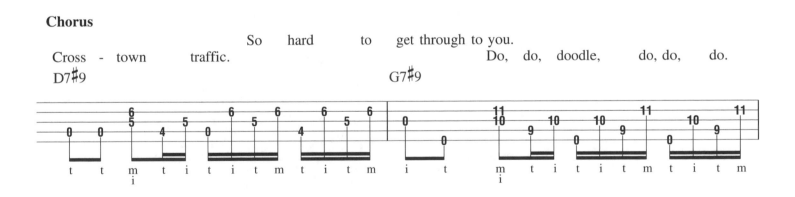

I don't need to run over you.

Cross - town traffic. Do, do, do, do, do, do.

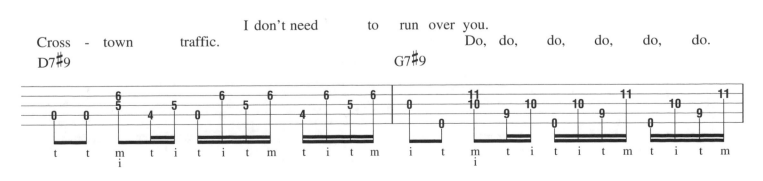

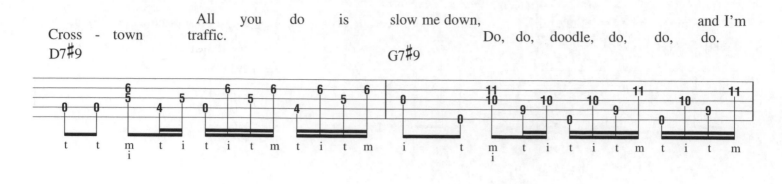

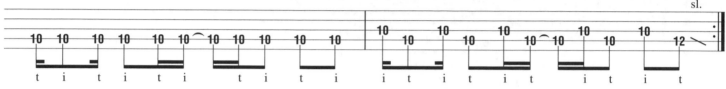

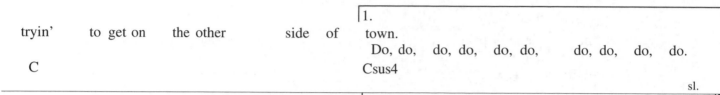

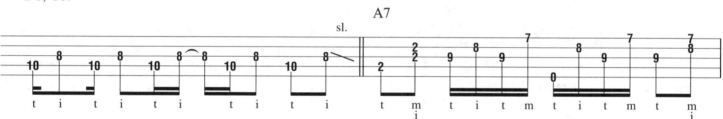

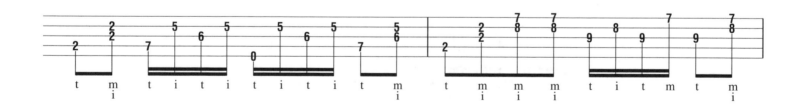

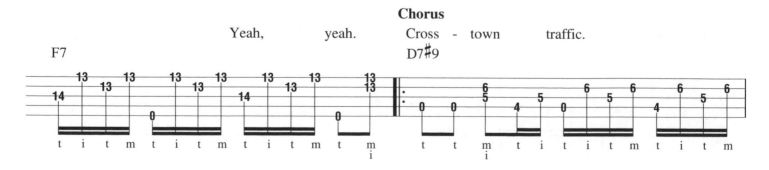

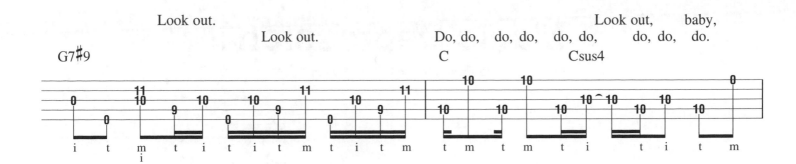

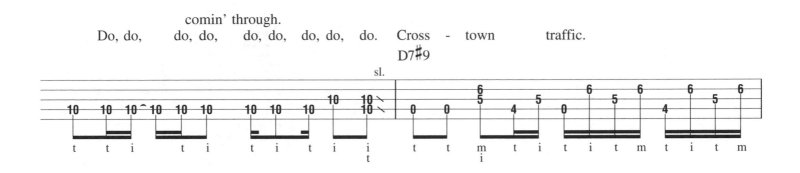

*Repeat & fade*

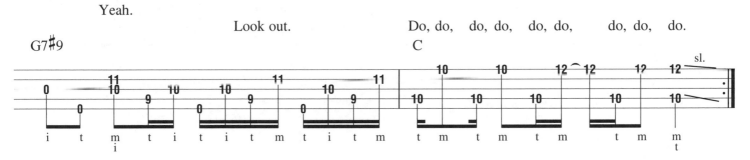

**Additional Lyrics**

Verse 2  I'm not the only soul
Who's accused of hit and run.
Tire tracks all across your back.
I can see you had your fun.
But, ah, darlin', can't you see
My signals turn from green to red?
And with you, I can see
A traffic jam ahead.

Chorus 2  You're just like…
Crosstown traffic.
So hard to get through to you.
Crosstown traffic…
I don't need to run over you.
Crosstown traffic…
All you do is slow me down,
An' I got better things on the
Other side of town.

# Manic Depression

**Words and Music by Jimi Hendrix**

G tuning:
(5th-1st) G-D-G-B-D

Key of G

**Intro**
**Moderately fast**

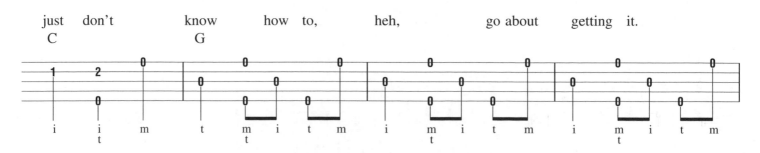

Feel - ing,  sweet feeling,          drops from my

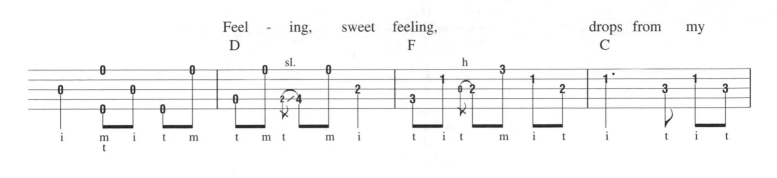

fingers,          fingers.                    Man - ic de -

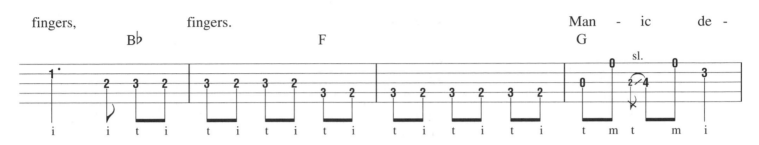

*To Coda* ⊕

pression's,          a,   cap - tured my  soul.          Yeah.

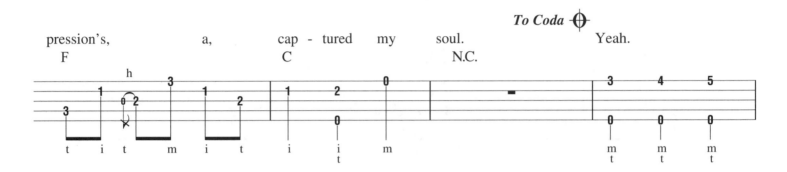

**Verse**

2. Wom - an  so

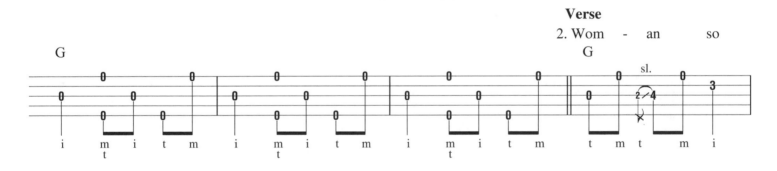

willing          the  sweet cause  in  vain.

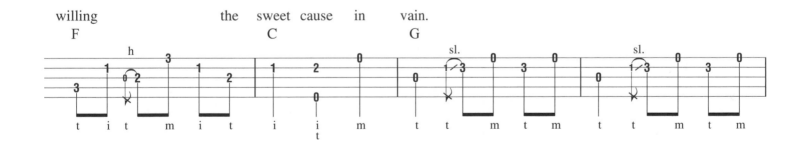

You  make love,  you  break  love,  it's a,

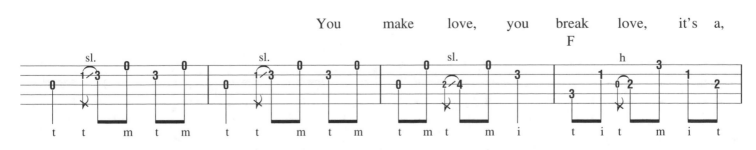

all       the       same              when it's,                    when it's    over.
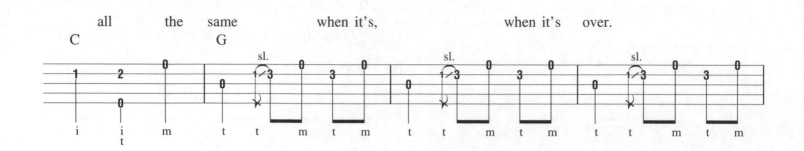

Mu - sic,   sweet   music,                     I    wish    I    could
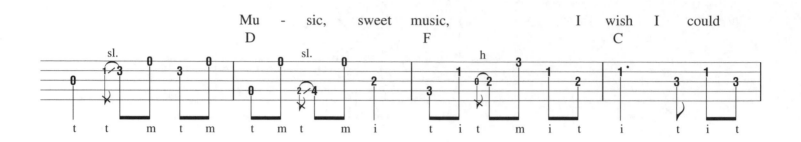

caress,       caress,                  caress.                     Man - ic   de -
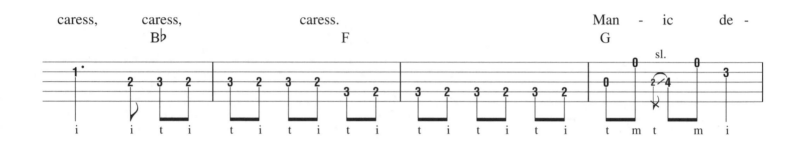

pression's       a            frus - trat - ing    mess.
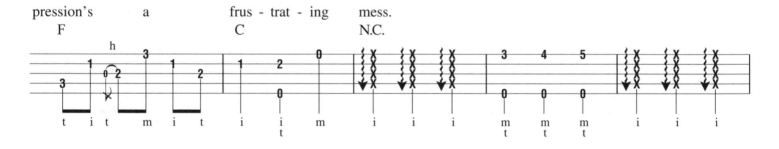

**Interlude**
Do,                                               do,
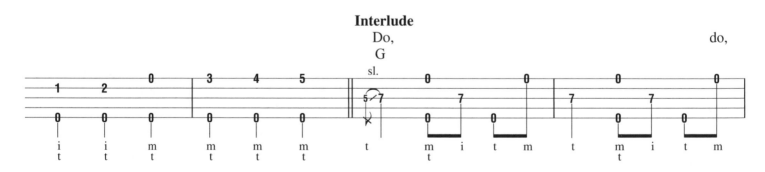

do,                                    do,
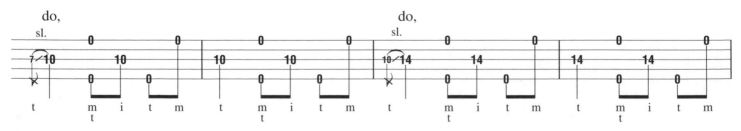

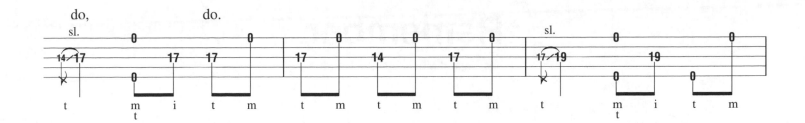

*D.S. al Coda*

$\oplus$ **Coda**

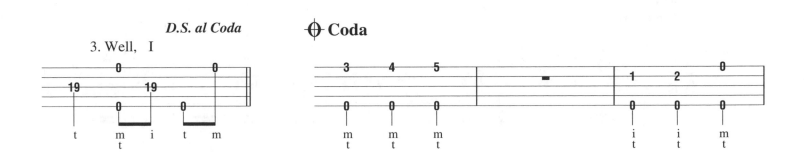

**Additional Lyrics**

3. Well, I thnk I'll go turn myself off and go on down.
All the way down.
Really ain't no use in me hanging around in
Your kind of scene.
Music, sweet music,
I wish I could caress and kiss.
Manic depression's a frustrating mess.

# Remember

**Words and Music by Jimi Hendrix**

G tuning:
(5th-1st) G-D-G-B-D

Key of A

**Intro**
**Moderately**

1. Oh, re -

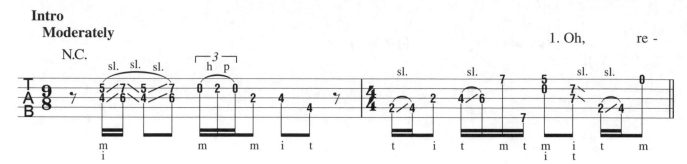

**Verse**

member the mockingbird, my baby bun. He used to
2. *See additional lyrics*

A

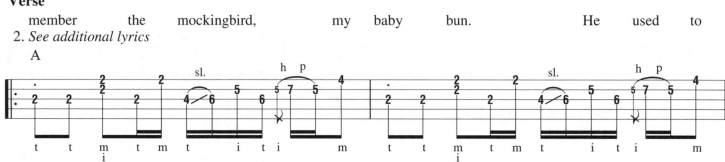

sing for his supper, ba - by. Yes, he used to

E

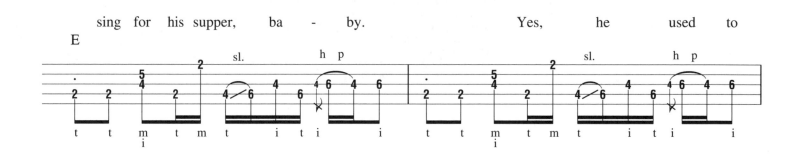

sing for his dinner, babe. He used to

D

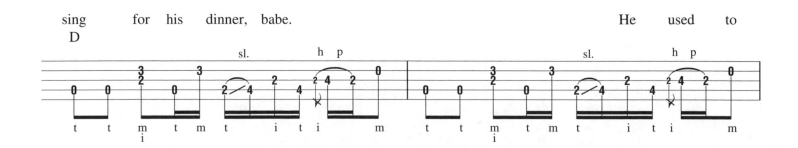

sing    so    sweet           but, a, since my baby      left    me,         he

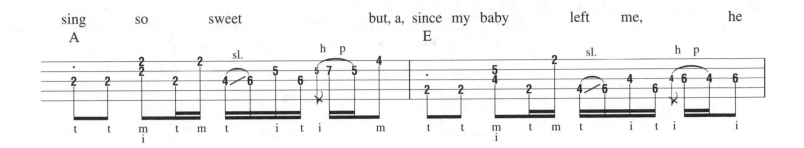

ain't    sang   a   tune     all       day.

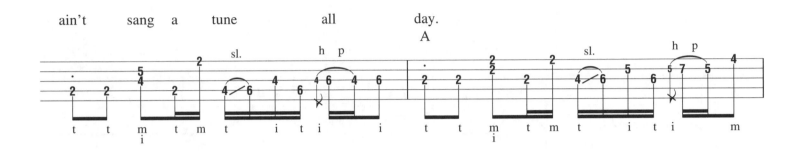

2. Oh,          re  -  mem -

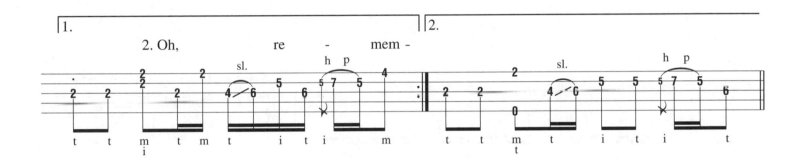

**Bridge**

Hey,        pretty ba - by,              come on     back   to me,

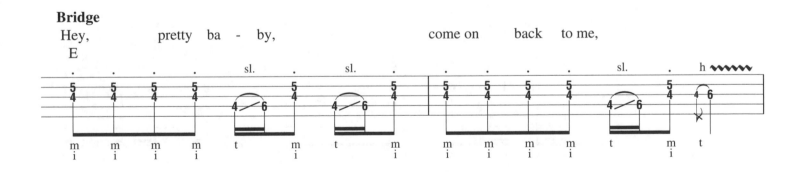

make everybod - y            hap - py   as   can   be,     yeah!

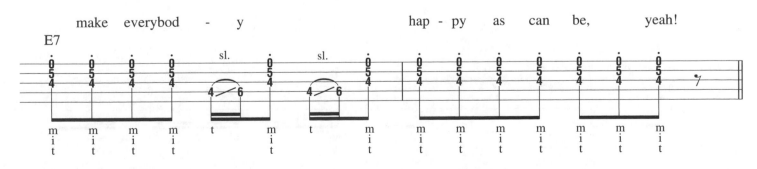

Key of B
**Banjo Solo**

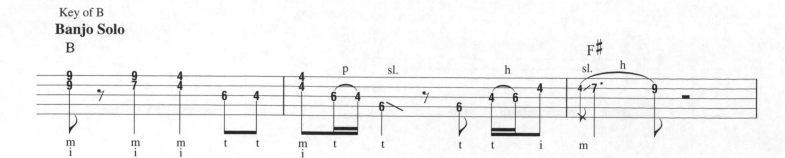

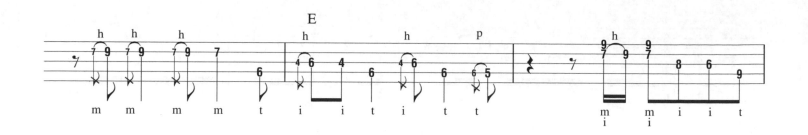

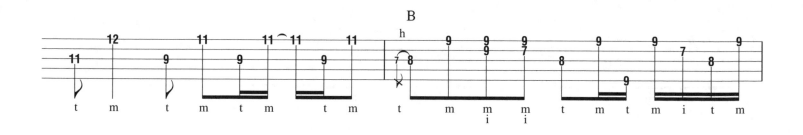

**Verse**

3. So,     baby,             if    you'll   please       come

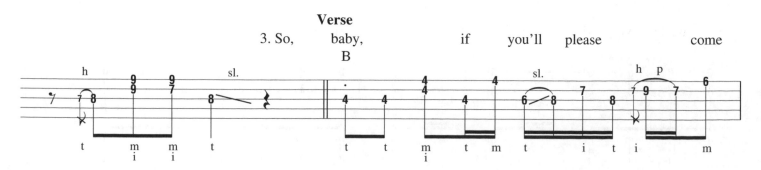

home again,        you know I'll    kiss you for my   supper.

F#

Yeah.       You know I'll   kiss you for my   dinner, baby,      now.

E

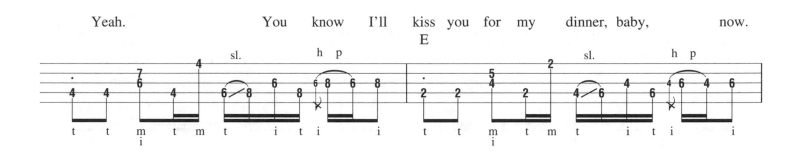

But,   uh,      if you don't come  back,  you know I'll

B

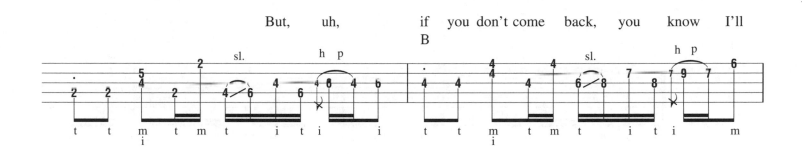

have to starve to death,       'cos I  ain't had a     kiss all  day,

F#

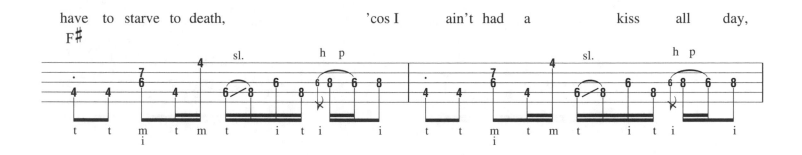

now.        Ah, babe.

B

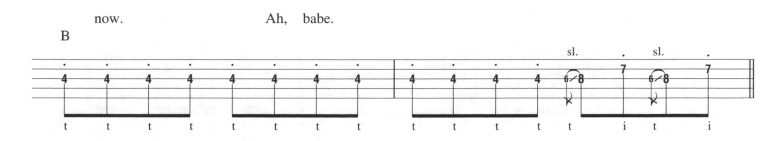

**Verse**

4. Please              re - member.

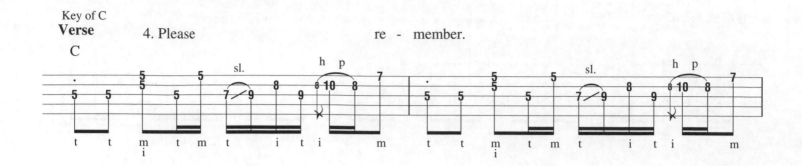

Got      to      remem - ber.                Yeah!

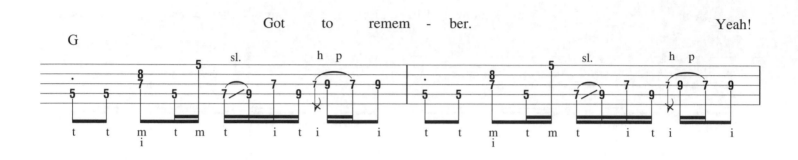

Got      to      remem - ber our love.

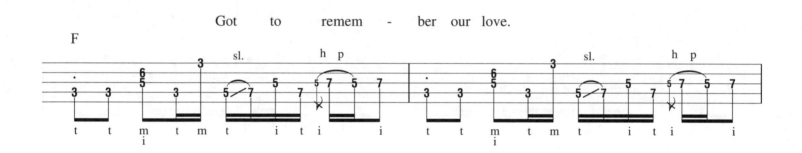

Come on back in, uh,           come on     back in my arms.

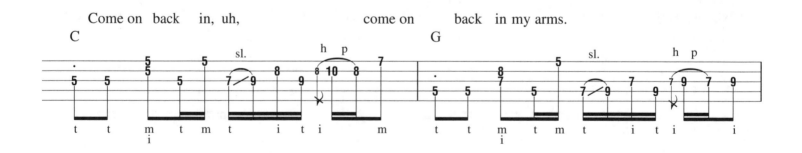

Make      everything         that     better.

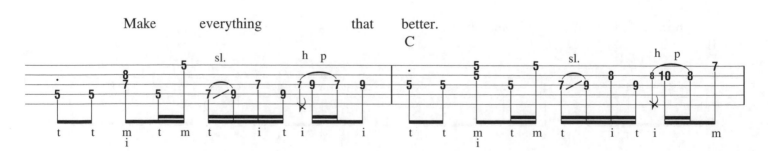

**Outro**

Aw, baby   hurry up now.

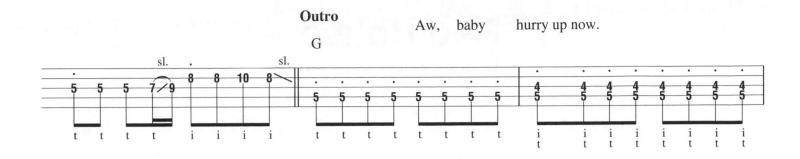

Can you hear me   calling you   back again   now?                                    C'mon, baby!

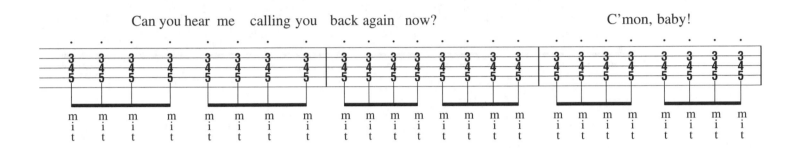

Stop   jivin' around!                              Hurry home,        hurry home.

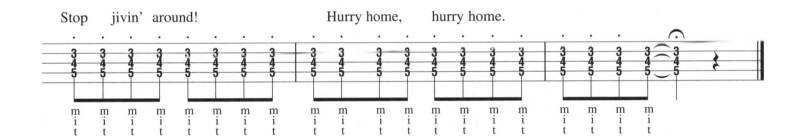

**Additional Lyrics**

2. Oh, remember the bluebirds and the honeybees,
   They used to sing for the sunshine.
   Yes, they used to sing for the honey, baby.
   They used to sing so sweet,
   But, a, since my baby left me,
   They ain't sing a tune all day.

# Red House

**Words and Music by Jimi Hendrix**

G tuning:
(5th-1st) G-D-G-B-D

Key of D

**Intro**
**Slow**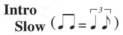

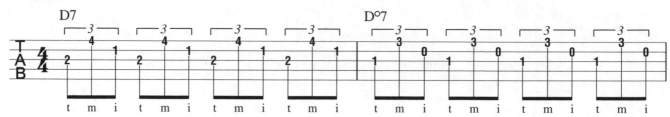

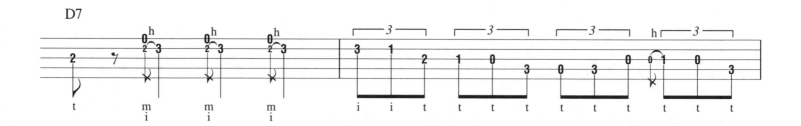

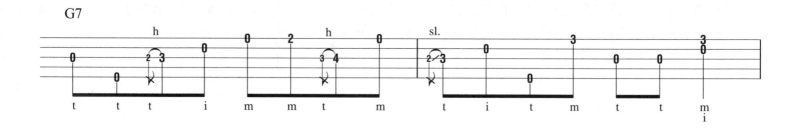

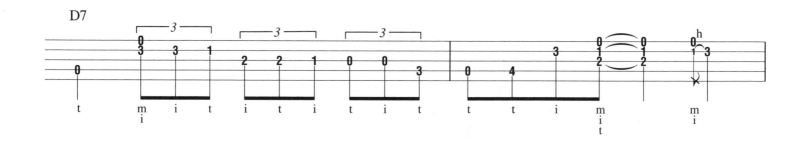

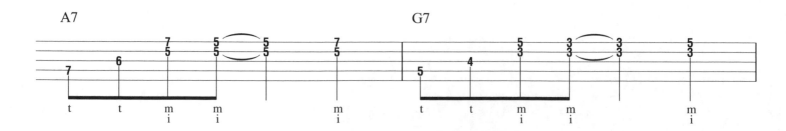

1. There's a

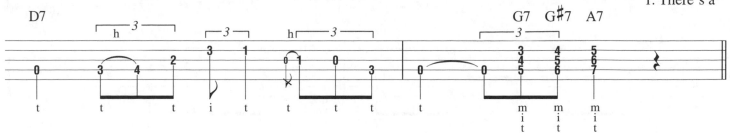

**$ Verse**

red house      over      yonder,           that's    where    my    baby    stays.

2., 3. *See additional lyrics*

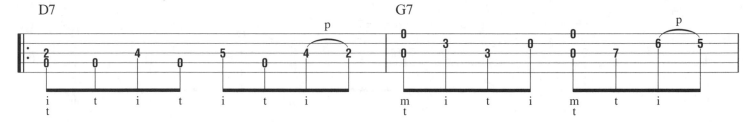

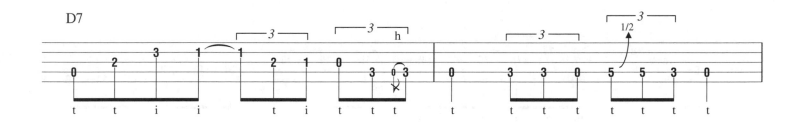

Lord, there's a red house over yonder,           Lord,   that's where my baby stays.

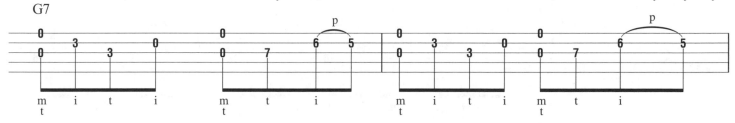

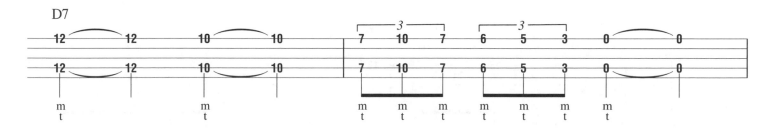

*To Coda* ⊕

I ain't been home to see    my baby           in ninety-nine and one-half   days.

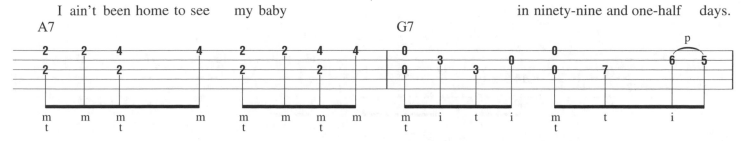

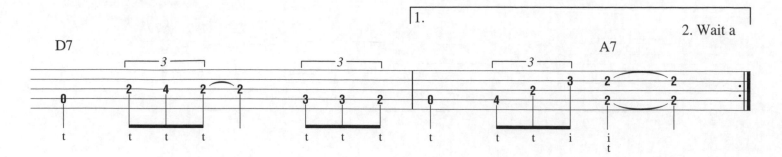

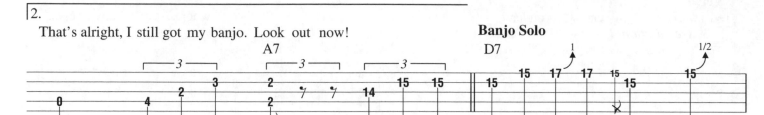

**2.**

That's alright, I still got my banjo. Look out now!

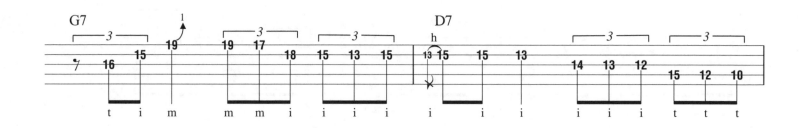

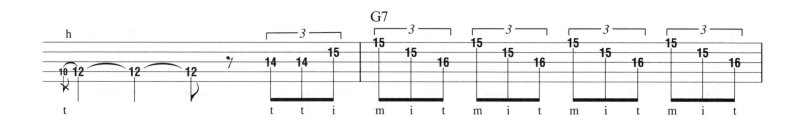

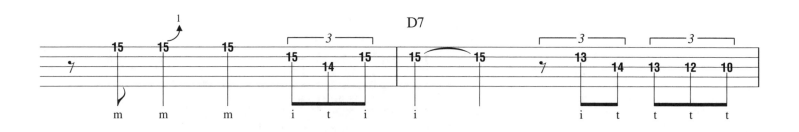

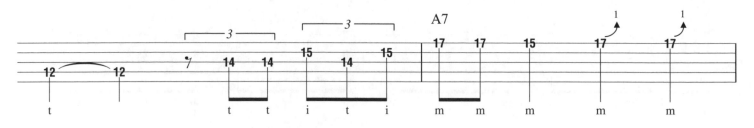

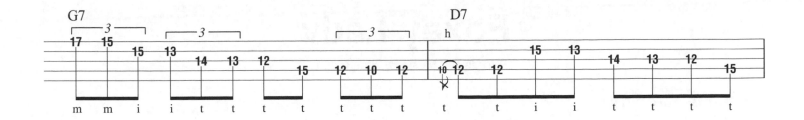

**_D.S. al Coda_**

3. Well, I might as well

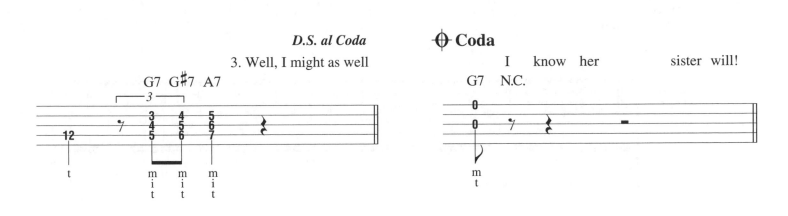

**⊕ Coda**

I know her          sister will!

**Outro**

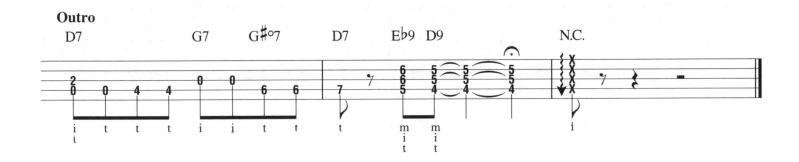

**Additional Lyrics**

2. Wait a minute, something's wrong here,
   The key won't unlock this door.
   Wait a minute, something's wrong here,
   Lord, have mercy, this key won't unlock this door.
   *Somthing's goin' wrong here.*
   I have a bad, bad feelin'
   That my baby don't live here no more.

3. Well, I might as well go back over yonder,
   Way back among the hills.
   *Yeah, that's what I'm gonna do.*
   Lord, I might as well go back over yonder,
   Way back yonder 'cross the hill.
   'Cos if my baby don't love me no more,
   I know her sister will.

# Foxey Lady

Words and Music by Jimi Hendrix

G tuning:
(5th-1st) G-D-G-B-D

Key of E

**Intro**
**Moderately**

N.C.
*cresc.*

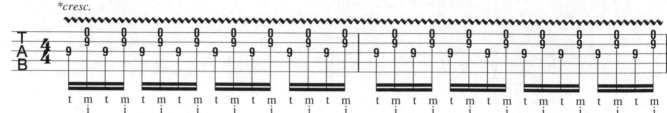

*Begin quietly, gradually getting louder (next 4 meas.)

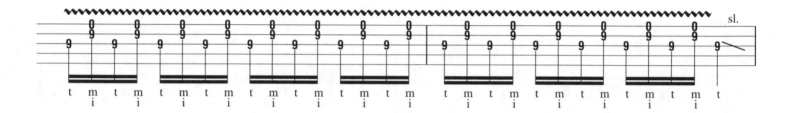

*Whispered: Foxey!*

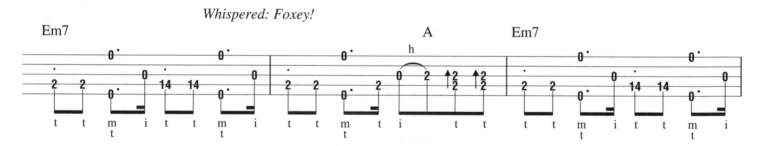

**Verse**

*Foxey!*

1. Uh, you know you are a cute little heartbreaker,
2. *See addional lyrics*

ha! *Foxey!* Yeah. And you know you are a

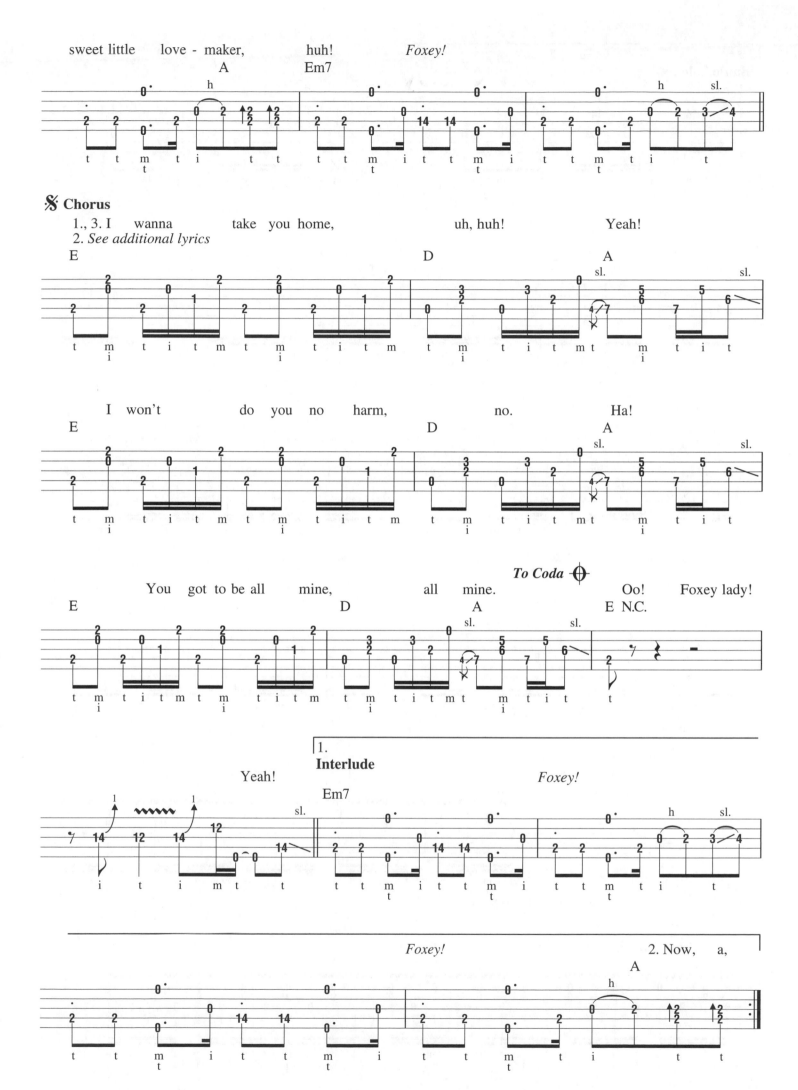

**Banjo Solo**

Em7

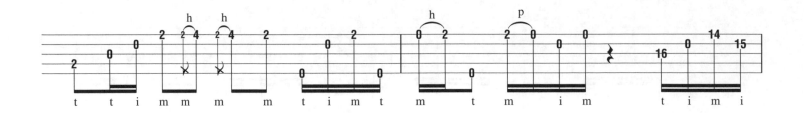

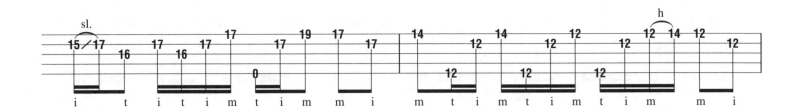

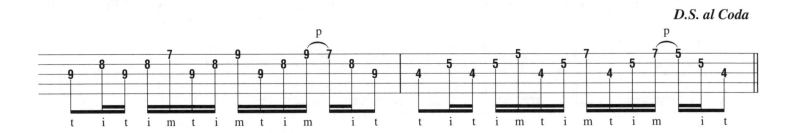

*D.S. al Coda*

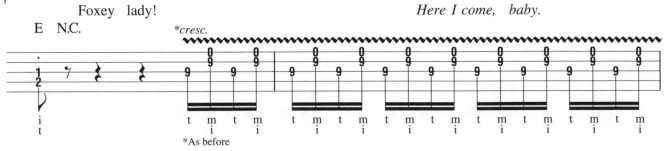

**⊕ Coda**

Foxey lady! *Here I come, baby.*

E   N.C.

*cresc.*

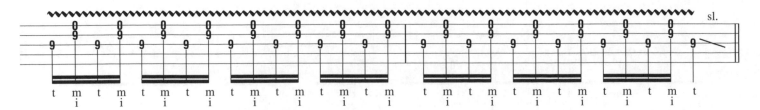

*As before

I'm   comin'   to   get   ya.

54

**Outro**

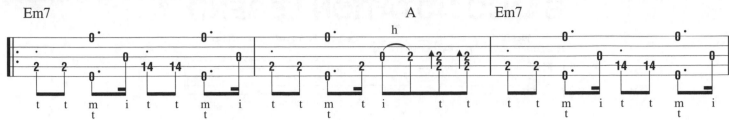

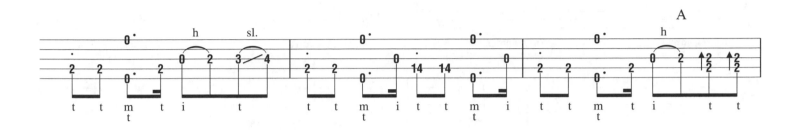

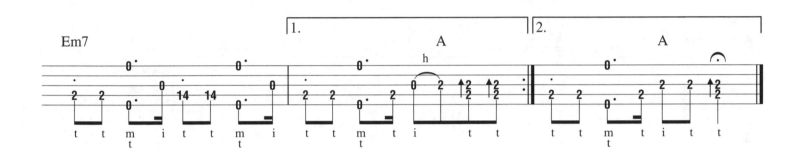

**Additional Lyrics**

Verse 2   Now, a, I see you, heh, come down on the scene.
            Oh, foxey!
            You make me wanna get up and scream.
            *Foxey!*
            Oh, baby, listen, now.

Chorus 2  I've made up my mind, yeah!
            I'm tired of wasting all my precious time.
            You've got to be all mine, all mine.
            Foxey lady!
            Here I come!

# BANJO NOTATION LEGEND

**TABLATURE** graphically represents the banjo fingerboard. Each horizontal line represents a string, and each number represents a fret.

Strings:
1 D
2 B
3 G
4 D
5 G

4th string, 2nd fret

1st & 2nd strings open, played together

**TIME SIGNATURE:**
The upper number indicates the number of beats per measure, the lower number indicates that a quarter note gets one beat.

**CUT TIME:**
Each note's time value should be cut in half. As a result, the music will be played twice as fast as it is written.

**QUARTER NOTE:**
time value = 1 beat

**EIGHTH NOTES:**
time value = 1/2 beat each

single    in series

**SIXTEENTH NOTES:**
time value = 1/4 beat each

single    in series

**DOTTED QUARTER NOTE:**
time value = 1 1/2 beat

**TIE:** Pick the 1st note only, then let it sustain for the combined time value.

**TRIPLET:** Three notes played in the same time normally occupied by two notes of the same time value.

**GRACE NOTE:** A quickly played note with no time value of its own. The grace note and the note following it only occupy the time value of the second note.

**RITARD:** A gradual slowing of the tempo or speed of the song.

**QUARTER REST:**
time value = 1 beat of silence

**EIGHTH REST:**
time value = 1/2 beat of silence

**HALF REST:**
time value = 2 beats of silence

**WHOLE REST:**
time value = 4 beats of silence

**ENDINGS:** When a repeated section has a first and second ending, play the first ending only the first time and play the second ending only the second time.

**REPEAT SIGNS:** Play the music between the repeat signs two times.

1.    2.

**D.S. AL CODA:**
Play through the music until you complete the measure labeled *"D.S. al Coda,"* then go back to the sign (𝄋). Then play until you complete the measure labeled *"To Coda ⊕,"* then skip to the section labeled *"⊕ Coda."*

𝄋

*To Coda* ⊕          *D.S. al Coda*          ⊕ *Coda*

**HAMMER-ON:** Strike the first (lower) note with one finger, then sound the higher note (on the same string) with another finger by fretting it without picking.

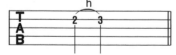

**PULL-OFF:** Place both fingers on the notes to be sounded. Strike the first note and without picking, pull the finger off to sound the second (lower) note.

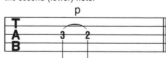

**SLIDE UP:** Strike the first note and then slide the same fret-hand finger up to the second note. The second note is not struck.

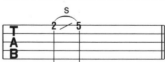

**SLIDE DOWN:** Strike the first note and then slide the same fret-hand finger down to the second note. The second note is not struck.

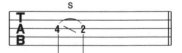

**HALF-STEP CHOKE:** Strike the note and bend the string up 1/2 step.

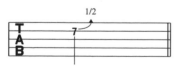

**WHOLE-STEP CHOKE:** Strike the note and bend the string up one step.

**NATURAL HARMONIC:** Strike the note while the fret-hand lightly touches the string directly over the fret indicated.

Harm.

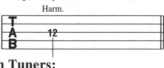

**BRUSH:** Play the notes of the chord indicated by quickly rolling them from bottom to top.

## Scruggs/Keith Tuners:

**HALF-TWIST UP:** Strike the note, twist tuner up 1/2 step, and continue playing.

**HALF-TWIST DOWN:** Strike the note, twist tuner down 1/2 step, and continue playing.

**WHOLE-TWIST UP:** Strike the note, twist tuner up one step, and continue playing.

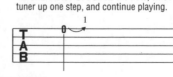

**WHOLE-TWIST DOWN:** Strike the note, twist tuner down one step, and continue playing.

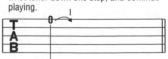

## Right Hand Fingerings

t = thumb          i = index finger          m = middle finger